UNITED NATIONS CONFERENCE ON TRADE AND DEVELOPMENT

HANDBOOK OF
STATISTICS
2022

United Nations

Geneva, 2022

Requests to reproduce excerpts or to photocopy should be addressed to the Copyright Clearance Center at copyright.com.

All other queries on rights and licences, including subsidiary rights, should be addressed to:

United Nations Publications
405 East 42nd Street
New York, New York 10017
United States of America
Email: publications@un.org
Website: https://shop.un.org/

The designations employed and the presentation of material on any map in this work do not imply the expression of any opinion whatsoever on the part of the United Nations concerning the legal status of any country, territory, city or area or of its authorities, or concerning the delimitation of its frontiers or boundaries.

A dispute exists between the Governments of Argentina and the United Kingdom of Great Britain and Northern Ireland concerning sovereignty over the Falkland Islands (Malvinas).

The final boundary between the Sudan and South Sudan has not yet been determined.

This publication has not been formally edited.

United Nations publication issued by the United Nations Conference on Trade and Development

TD/STAT.47

ISBN: 978-92-1-113076-8
eISBN: 978-92-1-002178-4
ISSN: 1992-8408
eISSN: 2225-3270
Sales No. E.22.II.D.45

Notes

The tables in this handbook represent extractions from or analytical summaries of datasets contained in the UNCTADstat Data Centre, available at:

https://unctadstat.unctad.org/

UNCTADstat is continuously updated and enhanced, thus providing users with the latest available statistics. Consequently, the figures from this handbook, which presents statistics at a point in time, may not always correspond with the latest figures in UNCTADstat.

Basic information on concepts, definitions and calculation methods of the presented statistics are provided in the boxes titled "Concepts and definitions" in each section and in annex 6.3 of this handbook. More detailed information on the sources and methods used for production of data available in UNCTADstat can be found in the documentation attached to the respective UNCTADstat dataset (UNCTAD, 2022a).

Where the designation "economy" appears, it refers to a country, territory or area. The assignment of economies to specific groups is done for statistical convenience and does not imply any assumption regarding the political or other affiliation of these economies by the United Nations. Likewise, the designations "developing" and "developed" are intended for statistical convenience and do not necessarily express a judgement about the stage reached by a particular economy in the development process.

Due to the removal of the group of the "transition economies" in the 2021 edition, and due to a reclassification of the development status of the Republic of Korea in 2022, the classification of economies into "developing" and "developed" applied in this handbook is different from the classification used in earlier editions. Also, a broader definition of small island developing States (SIDS) as defined by the United Nations Office of the High Representative for the Least Developed Countries, Landlocked Developing Countries and Small Island Developing States (UN-OHRLLS) is applied since 2021. The corresponding group aggregates are therefore not comparable with data presented in earlier handbooks. For more details, see annex 6.2 of this handbook.

The population data used in this edition have been substantially revised by the United Nations Population Department in summer 2022. They reflect for the first time the effects of the COVID-19 pandemic. This had an impact on the figures of gross domestic product (GDP) per capita.

Unless otherwise specified, the values of groups of economies represent the sums of the values of the individual economies included in the group. Calculation of these aggregates may take into account data estimated by the UNCTAD secretariat that are not necessarily reported separately. When data coverage is insufficient within a group of economies, no aggregation is undertaken and the symbol (-) is assigned.

Due to rounding, values do not necessarily add up exactly to their corresponding totals.

United States dollars (US$) are expressed in current United States dollars of the year to which they refer, unless otherwise specified. "Ton" means metric ton (1 000 kg).

Due to space constraints, the names of the following countries may appear in abbreviated form: the Plurinational State of Bolivia, the Democratic People's Republic of Korea, the Democratic Republic of the Congo, the Islamic Republic of Iran, Lao People's Democratic Republic, the Federated States of Micronesia, the United Kingdom of Great Britain and Northern Ireland, and the Bolivarian Republic of Venezuela.

The UNCTAD Handbook of Statistics 2022 is available in PDF format from the UNCTAD website, at https://unctad.org/HandbookOfStatistics. The e-handbook is available at https://hbs.unctad.org.

The world by development status

- Developing economies
- Developed economies
- /// Least developed countries (LDCs)

The boundaries and names shown and the designations used on this map do not imply official endorsement or acceptance by the United Nations.

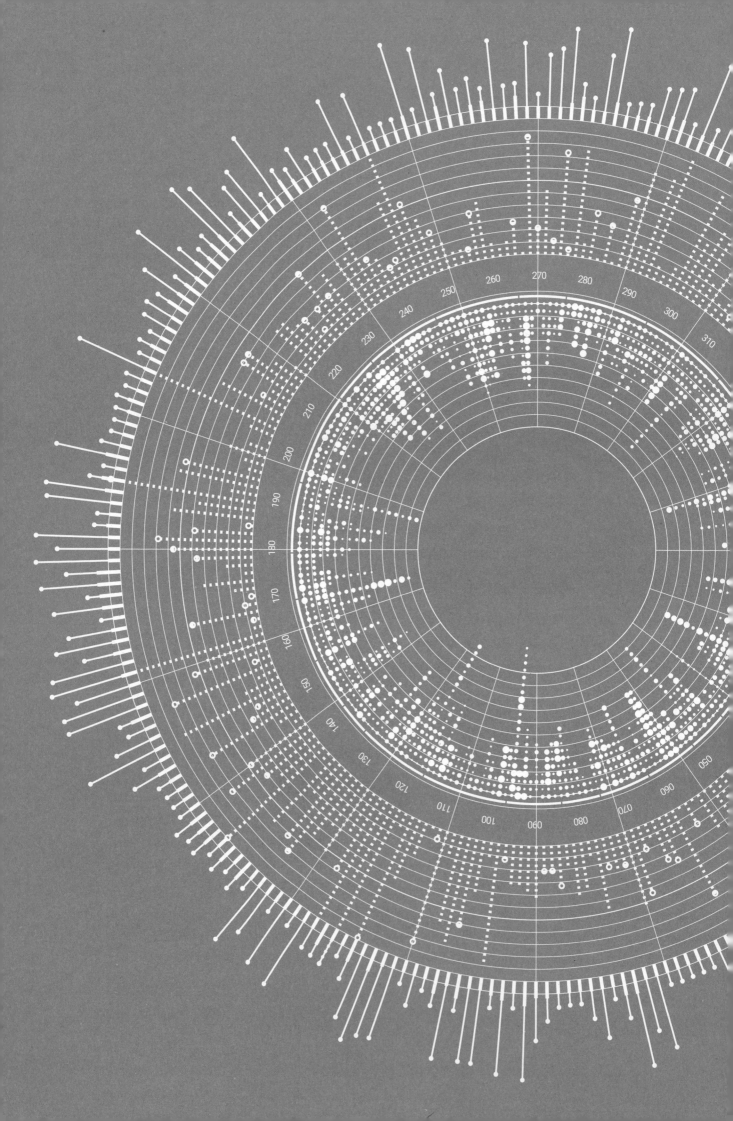

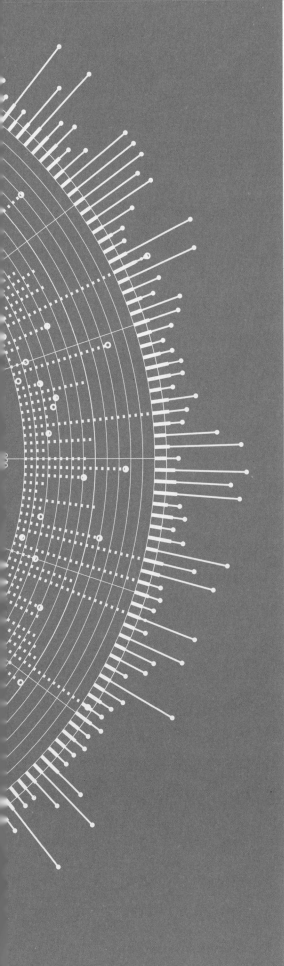

TABLE OF **CONTENTS**

Maps and Figures

Figures

Tables

Introduction

The UNCTAD Handbook of Statistics 2022 provides a wide range of statistics and indicators relevant to the analysis of international trade, economy, investment, maritime transport, and development overall. It comes at a time of cascading crises that overlap and compound each other. In uncertain times, reliable statistical information becomes even more indispensable for effective policy responses and decisions, aiding countries to recover from the crises and build a more just, inclusive, and sustainable economy.

The UNCTAD Handbook of Statistics and the UNCTADstat Data Centre make internationally comparable data sets available to policymakers, specialists, researchers, officials of national Governments, representatives of international organizations, journalists, executive managers, and experts of non-governmental organizations. In addition, these statistics underpin all UNCTAD activities. Whether for research, policy advice or technical cooperation, UNCTAD needs reliable and internationally comparable trade, financial and macroeconomic data with global coverage, spanning several decades.

The 2021 data show a strong rebound of GDP, international trade, maritime transport, foreign direct investment (FDI) and other spheres of global economic activity. While global merchandise trade exceeded its pre-pandemic level by far, for trade in services the recovery in 2021 was not strong enough to compensate the dramatic fall in 2020 experienced during the outbreak of the COVID-19 pandemic, especially in travel. However, UNCTAD nowcasts suggest that the rebound is continuing in 2022, albeit at a slightly moderated speed, leading to new record highs in both goods and services trade values.

The 2022 nowcasts on global merchandise and services trade included in this handbook represent annualized snapshots of UNCTAD's quarterly nowcasts, which are updated weekly. New this year is their publication to a dedicated dashboard on UNCTADstat, which allows tracking the development of the nowcast and their drivers in almost 'real time'; see https://unctadstat.unctad.org/EN/Nowcasts.html.

This year again, the online edition of the handbook, the e-handbook, incorporates interactive charts and maps at: https://hbs.unctad.org/. The e-handbook, including its maps and charts, is an interactive tool and provides readers with direct access to the data at the UNCTADstat Data Centre from each table, map and chart.

Abbreviations

BPM6	Balance of Payments and International Investment Position Manual, Sixth Edition
BRICS	Brazil, Russia, India, China and South Africa
CIF	cost, insurance and freight
CPI	consumer price index
Dem. Rep.	Democratic Republic
dwt	dead-weight tons
EBOPS 2010	2010 Extended Balance of Payments Services Classification
FDI	foreign direct investment
FOB	free on board
G20	Group of Twenty
GDP	gross domestic product
GFCF	gross fixed capital formation
gt	gross tons
HIPCs	heavily indebted poor countries
HS	Harmonized Commodity Description and Coding System
IMF	International Monetary Fund
ISIC	International Standard Industrial Classification of All Economic Activities
LDCs	least developed countries
LLDCs	landlocked developing countries
LNG	liquefied natural gas
LPG	liquefied petroleum gas
LSBCI	liner shipping bilateral connectivity index
LSCI	liner shipping connectivity index
Rep.	Republic
SAR	Special Administrative Region
SIDS	small island developing States
SITC	Standard International Trade Classification
TEU	twenty-foot equivalent unit
UCPI	UNCTAD Commodity Price Index
UN-OHRLLS	United Nations Office of the High Representative for the Least Developed Countries, Landlocked Developing Countries and Small Island Developing States
US$	United States dollars
WTO	World Trade Organization

Symbols

0	Zero means that the amount is nil or negligible.
_	The symbol underscore indicates that the item is not applicable.
..	Two dots indicate that the data are not available or are not separately reported.
-	The use of a hyphen on data area means that data is estimated and included in the aggregations but not published.

An en dash between years (e.g. "1985–1990") signifies the full period involved, including the initial and final years.

(e)	Estimate
(u)	Preliminary estimate

1

INTERNATIONAL MERCHANDISE TRADE

KEY FIGURES **2021**

Value of
world merchandise
exports
US$22.3 trillion

Change of
world merchandise
exports

+26.5%

LDCs' share in
global exports

1.05%

NOWCAST **2022**

Growth of global
merchandise exports

+13.8%

1.1 Total merchandise trade

Map 1.1 Merchandise exports as a ratio to gross domestic product, 2021
(Percentage)

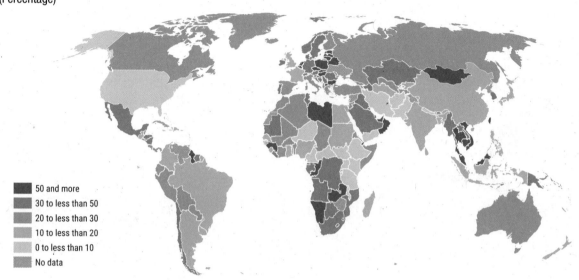

50 and more
30 to less than 50
20 to less than 30
10 to less than 20
0 to less than 10
No data

Concepts and definitions

The figures on international merchandise trade in this chapter measure the value of goods which add or subtract from the stock of material resources of an economy by entering or leaving its territory (United Nations, 2011). This definition is slightly different from the definition of trade in goods in the balance-of-payments framework (see section 3.2).

The value of exports is mostly recorded as the free-on-board (FOB) value, whereas the value of imports includes cost, insurance and freight (CIF).

The trade balance is calculated as the difference between the values of exports and imports.

Merchandise trade figures from 2014 to 2021, at total product level with partner world, are jointly produced by UNCTAD and the World Trade Organization (WTO).

Strong post-pandemic recovery

In 2021, the value of world merchandise exports increased strongly, by 26.5 per cent, after two consecutive years of decline. Global exports amounted to US$22.3 trillion, US$3.3 trillion higher than the pre-pandemic value recorded two years before, in 2019. In 2022, the exports value is nowcast to continue growing, at a rate of 13.8 per cent from 2021.

Higher merchandise exports were recorded in the 'North' than in the 'South', in 2021. Developing economies contributed US$9.9 trillion and developed economies US$12.4 trillion to the world total. Asia and Oceania accounted for 45 per cent of global merchandise exports, followed by Europe with 37 per cent and America with 16 per cent. Africa remained underrepresented, capturing only 2 per cent of the global market.

Figure 1.1.1 World merchandise exports
(Trillions of United States dollars)

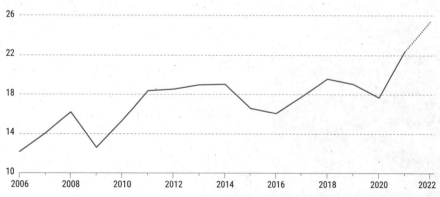

Note: The dotted line indicates UNCTAD nowcasts. For the weekly update of the nowcast and its methodology, see UNCTAD (2022b).

Trade upswing in all regions

In 2021, merchandise exports and imports increased considerably in all groups of economies classified by development status: between 23 and 42 per cent.

Developing economies in Africa experienced the highest rise in exports (+42.2 per cent), followed by developed economies in Asia and Oceania (+30.2 per cent). In terms of imports, developing economies in the Americas registered the highest increase (+38.1 per cent). They were followed by developing economies in Asia and Oceania (+30.2 per cent).

Figure 1.1.2 Merchandise trade annual growth rates, 2021
(Percentage)

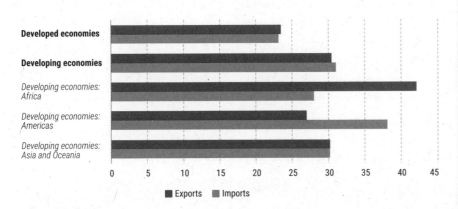

Increase in exports of 13.8% nowcast for 2022

In 2021, world merchandise trade increased strongly: by 26.5%

Development of trade imbalances

Developing economies registered a considerable increase in their trade surplus in 2021 for the second consecutive year. Their trade balance stood at +US$535 in 2020 and reached +US$650 billion in 2021.

By contrast, developed economies witnessed a continuously rising merchandise trade deficit over recent years. It was recorded at US$909 billion in 2021. During that year, the developed world's exports declined more than imports.

Developing economies' imports in 2021 followed the global trend.

Up by 31%

Figure 1.1.3 Merchandise trade balance
(Billions of United States dollars)

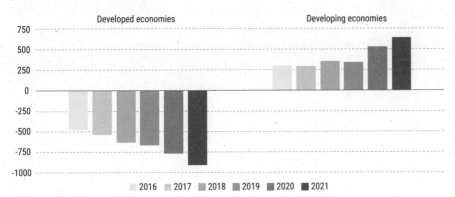

Note: Trade balances do not add up to zero at world level due to CIF included in imports and cross-country differences in compilation methods.

US$909 billion trade deficit

recorded by developed economies in 2021

Table 1.1.1 | Merchandise trade by group of economies

Group of economies	Exports Value (Millions of US$)		Exports Annual growth rate (Percentage)	Imports Value (Millions of US$)		Imports Annual growth rate (Percentage)	Trade balance Value (Millions of US$)	Trade balance Ratio to imports (Percentage)
	2020	2021	2021	2020	2021	2021	2021	2021
World	**17 648**	**22 328**	**26.5**	**17 879**	**22 587**	**26.3**	**-258**	**-1.1**
Developed economies	10 045	12 410	23.6	10 810	13 319	23.2	-909	-6.8
Developing economies	7 604	9 918	30.4	7 069	9 267	31.1	650	7.0
Developing economies: Africa	394	561	42.2	491	629	28.1	-68	-10.8
Developing economies: Americas	951	1 208	27.0	917	1 267	38.1	-58	-4.6
Developing economies: Asia and Oceania	6 258	8 149	30.2	5 660	7 372	30.2	777	10.5
Selected groups								
Developing economies excluding China	5 014	6 554	30.7	5 003	6 579	31.5	-25	-0.4
Developing economies excluding LDCs	7 419	9 683	30.5	6 823	8 956	31.3	727	8.1
LDCs	185	235	26.9	246	311	26.6	-76	-24.5
LLDCs	168	219	30.3	206	250	21.7	-31	-12.4
SIDS (UN-OHRLLS)	419	531	26.7	418	515	23.2	16	3.1
HIPCs (IMF)	136	176	29.4	164	204	23.9	-27	-13.5
BRICS	3 495	4 657	33.3	2 929	3 914	33.6	743	19.0
G20	13 569	17 067	25.8	13 799	17 368	25.9	-301	-1.7

Table 1.1.2 | Merchandise trade of least developed countries, main exporters

Economy[a]	Exports Value (Millions of US$)		Exports Annual growth rate (Percentage)	Imports Value (Millions of US$)		Imports Annual growth rate (Percentage)	Trade balance Value (Millions of US$)	Trade balance Ratio to imports (Percentage)
	2020	2021	2021	2020	2021	2021	2021	2021
LDCs	**185 210**	**235 103**	**26.9**	**245 924**	**311 426**	**26.6**	**-76 323**	**-24.5**
LDCs: Africa and Haiti	107 708	145 459	35.0	127 020	151 982	19.7	-6 523	-4.3
Angola	20 937	33 581	60.4	9 543	11 795	23.6	21 787	184.7
Congo, Dem. Rep. of the	14 122	(e) 23 500	(e) 66.4	6 663	(e) 10 300	(e) 54.6	(e) 13 200	(e) 128.2
Zambia	7 821	11 141	42.4	5 323	7 096	33.3	4 045	57.0
Guinea	8 931	(e) 10 433	(e) 16.8	3 727	(e) 4 094	(e) 9.8	(e) 6 339	(e) 154.8
Tanzania, United Republic of	6 061	6 391	5.4	8 439	10 024	18.8	-3 634	-36.2
LDCs: Asia	76 816	88 592	15.3	117 214	157 305	34.2	-68 713	-43.7
Bangladesh	33 605	44 223	31.6	52 804	(e) 80 448	(e) 52.4	(e) -36 225	(e) -45.0
Cambodia	17 716	17 362	-2.0	19 114	28 369	48.4	-11 007	-38.8
Myanmar	16 692	15 145	-9.3	17 947	14 322	-20.2	823	5.7
Lao People's Dem. Rep.	6 115	7 695	25.8	5 370	6 275	16.8	1 419	22.6
Nepal	856	1 684	96.8	9 856	15 893	61.3	-14 208	-89.4
LDCs: Islands	686	1 051	53.2	1 689	2 139	26.6	-1 087	-50.8
Timor-Leste	264	616	133.6	625	873	39.5	-257	-29.5
Solomon Islands	379	371	-2.0	(e) 479	(e) 562	(e) 17.3	(e) -191	(e) -34.0
Comoros	21	34	66.8	280	328	17.0	-293	-89.5
Sao Tome and Principe	14	21	49.2	138	166	20.5	-145	-87.5
Kiribati	9	9	-1.6	133	176	32.2	-167	-94.8

[a] Ranked by value of exports 2021.

Table 1.1.3 | **Leading exporters and importers in developing economies, by group of economies, 2021**

Developing economies: Africa

Exporter (Ranked by value)	Value (Billions of US$)	Share in world total (Percentage)	Annual growth rate (Percentage)
South Africa	124	0.55	44.0
Nigeria	47	0.21	31.7
Egypt	44	0.20	63.8
Algeria	(e) 37	(e) 0.16	(e) 54.2
Morocco	36	0.16	32.0
Developing Africa	**561**	**2.51**	**42.2**

Importer (Ranked by value)	Value (Billions of US$)	Share in world total (Percentage)	Annual growth rate (Percentage)
South Africa	(e) 114	(e) 0.50	(e) 35.6
Egypt	84	0.37	39.5
Morocco	58	0.26	32.4
Nigeria	52	0.23	45.3
Algeria	(e) 36	(e) 0.16	(e) 4.7
Developing Africa	**629**	**2.78**	**28.1**

Developing economies: Americas

Exporter (Ranked by value)	Value (Billions of US$)	Share in world total (Percentage)	Annual growth rate (Percentage)
Mexico	495	2.22	18.6
Brazil	281	1.26	34.2
Chile	95	0.42	27.8
Argentina	78	0.35	42.0
Peru	59	0.27	50.1
Developing Americas	**1 208**	**5.41**	**27.0**

Importer (Ranked by value)	Value (Billions of US$)	Share in world total (Percentage)	Annual growth rate (Percentage)
Mexico	522	2.31	32.8
Brazil	235	1.04	41.1
Chile	92	0.41	55.7
Argentina	63	0.28	49.2
Colombia	61	0.27	40.5
Developing Americas	**1 267**	**5.61**	**38.1**

Developing economies: Asia and Oceania

Exporter (Ranked by value)	Value (Billions of US$)	Share in world total (Percentage)	Annual growth rate (Percentage)
China	3 364	15.07	29.9
China, Hong Kong SAR	670	3.00	22.1
Singapore	457	2.05	26.2
China, Taiwan Province of	448	2.01	28.9
United Arab Emirates	425	1.90	26.8
Developing Asia and Oceania	**8 149**	**36.50**	**30.2**

Importer (Ranked by value)	Value (Billions of US$)	Share in world total (Percentage)	Annual growth rate (Percentage)
China	2 689	11.90	30.1
China, Hong Kong SAR	712	3.15	25.0
India	573	2.54	53.5
Singapore	406	1.80	23.2
China, Taiwan Province of	382	1.69	32.6
Developing Asia and Oceania	**7 372**	**32.64**	**30.2**

1.2 Trade structure by partner

Map 1.2 Main world import flows, 2021
(Billions of United States dollars)

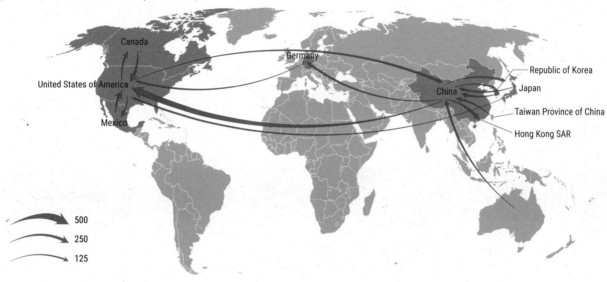

Note: Bilateral imports of US$125 billion or more are shown.

Concepts and definitions

Intra-trade is the trade between economies belonging to the same group. Extra-trade is the trade of economies of the same group with all economies outside the group. It represents the difference between a group's total trade and intra-trade.

The exports from an economy A to an economy B do not always equal the imports of economy B from economy A recorded FOB. The reasons for these trade asymmetries include: a conceptual difference between exporting economy and country of origin; different times of recording for exports and imports; different treatment of transit trade; underreporting; measurement errors; mis-pricing and mis-invoicing.

The exports to (imports from) all economies of the world do not always exactly add up to total exports (imports). The difference is caused by ship stores, bunkers and other exports of minor importance.

Main global trade patterns

The world's largest bilateral flows of merchandise trade run between China and the United States of America, and between their respective neighbouring economies. In 2021, goods worth US$542 billion were imported by the United States from China and US$181 billion by China from the United States. China's trade – exports and imports – with Hong Kong Special Administrative Region (SAR), Japan, Taiwan, Province of China, and the Republic of Korea totalled US$1.58 trillion. The United States' trade with Mexico and Canada was worth US$1.34 trillion.

Intra-regional trade was most pronounced in Europe. In 2021, 68 per cent of all European exports were to trading partners on the same continent. In Asia, this rate was 59 per cent. By contrast, in Oceania, Latin America and the Caribbean, Africa, and Northern America, most trade was extra-regional.

Figure 1.2.1 Intra- and extra-regional exports, 2021
(Percentage of total exports)

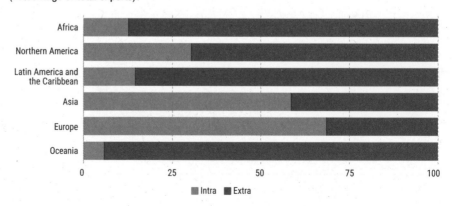

Trade within and between 'hemispheres'

In 2021, goods worth US$8.5 trillion were exchanged between developed economies (North-North trade), whereas merchandise trade among developing economies (South-South trade) amounted to US$5.4 trillion. Exports from developed to developing economies and vice-versa (North-South, and South-North trade) totaled US$8.0 trillion. Thus, for developed economies, trade with developing economies was slightly less important than trade within their own group.

Figure 1.2.2 Global trade flows, 2021

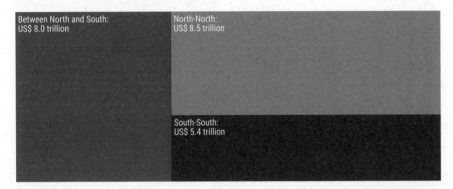

Note: North refers to developed economies, South to developing economies; trade is measured from the export side; deliveries to ship stores and bunkers as well as minor and special-category exports with unspecified destination are not included.

With whom do developing economies mainly trade?

In 2021, developing economies shipped most of their exports to the United States of America (US$1.6 trillion), followed by China (US$1.3 trillion) and other Asian economies. In terms of imports, China ranked number one (US$1.7 trillion) and was distantly followed by the United States of America (US$893 billion), with barely half of the value for China.

Exports from American developing economies were more oriented towards the Americas, especially to the United States of America (US$503 billion). For African developing economies, main export markets were in Asia, with China (US$93.7 billion) and India (US$42.5 billion) as the top destinations.

Figure 1.2.3 Developing economies' main export destinations, 2021
(Billions of United States dollars)

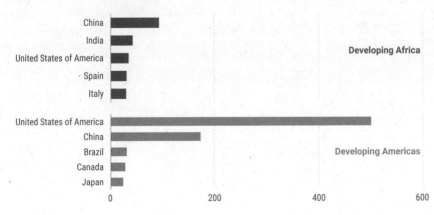

United States of America traded **US$1.3 trillion** with Canada and Mexico in 2021

59% of Asia's trade is intra-regional

The South still trades less with the South than with the North: US$8.0 trillion US$5.4 trillion

United States and China the main markets for developing economies' exports

Table 1.2.1 | **Exports by origin and destination, 2021**
(Billions of United States dollars)

Origin	Destination					
	World	Developed economies	Developing economies			
			Total	Africa	Americas	Asia and Oceania
World	**22 140**	**12 988**	**8 925**	**672**	**1 208**	**7 044**
	(100)	(59)	(40)	(3)	(5)	(32)
Developed economies	12 205	8 483	3 526	258	694	2 575
	(100)	(70)	(29)	(2)	(6)	(21)
Developing economies	9 935	4 506	5 398	414	515	4 470
	(100)	(45)	(54)	(4)	(5)	(45)
Developing economies: Africa	559	257	300	71	12	217
	(100)	(46)	(54)	(13)	(2)	(39)
Developing economies: Americas	1 206	713	467	19	175	273
	(100)	(59)	(39)	(2)	(15)	(23)
Developing economies: Asia and Oceania	8 170	3 535	4 631	324	327	3 979
	(100)	(43)	(57)	(4)	(4)	(49)

Note: Percentage of exports to the whole world in parentheses.

Table 1.2.2 | **Exports by origin and destination, selected years**
(Billions of United States dollars)

Origin	Year	Destination					
		World	Developed economies	Developing economies			
				Total	Africa	Americas	Asia and Oceania
World	2011	18 198	11 128	6 867	579	1 079	5 209
	2016	15 889	9 536	6 256	509	898	4 849
	2021	22 140	12 988	8 925	672	1 208	7 044
Developed economies	2011	10 691	7 487	3 052	277	634	2 141
	2016	9 278	6 456	2 757	224	569	1 964
	2021	12 205	8 483	3 526	258	694	2 575
Developing economies	2011	7 507	3 641	3 815	302	445	3 068
	2016	6 611	3 080	3 499	285	329	2 886
	2021	9 935	4 506	5 398	414	515	4 470
Developing economies: Africa	2011	621	344	263	81	26	156
	2016	358	167	185	67	8	111
	2021	559	257	300	71	12	217
Developing economies: Americas	2011	1 105	674	422	23	226	174
	2016	882	564	310	17	146	147
	2021	1 206	713	467	19	175	273
Developing economies: Asia and Oceania	2011	5 781	2 623	3 129	198	194	2 738
	2016	5 371	2 349	3 004	201	175	2 628
	2021	8 170	3 535	4 631	324	327	3 979

Table 1.2.3 | **Top destinations of developing economies' exports**

Destination (Ranked by value of exports)	Rank		2021		
	2021	2016	Value	Share in total exports	Cumulative share
			(Billions of US$)	(Percentage)	(Percentage)
United States of America	1	1	1 634	16.5	16.5
China	2	2	1 314	13.2	29.7
China, Hong Kong SAR	3	3	571	5.7	35.4
Japan	4	4	463	4.7	40.1
India	5	6	394	4.0	44.0
Korea, Republic of	6	5	349	3.5	47.6
Germany	7	7	253	2.5	50.1
Netherlands	8	9	239	2.4	52.5
Viet Nam	9	13	236	2.4	54.9
Singapore	10	8	221	2.2	57.1
China, Taiwan Province of	11	12	212	2.1	59.3
Malaysia	12	14	198	2.0	61.2
United Kingdom	13	10	194	2.0	63.2
United Arab Emirates	14	11	177	1.8	65.0
Thailand	15	15	177	1.8	66.8
Rest of the world			3 302	33.2	100.0
World			**9 935**	**100.0**	–

Table 1.2.4 | **Top origins of developing economies' imports**

Origin (Ranked by value of imports)	Rank		2021		
	2021	2016	Value	Share in total imports	Cumulative share
			(Billions of US$)	(Percentage)	(Percentage)
China	1	1	1 683	18.3	18.3
United States of America	2	2	893	9.7	27.9
Japan	3	3	524	5.7	33.6
Korea, Republic of	4	4	493	5.4	39.0
China, Taiwan Province of	5	6	471	5.1	44.1
Germany	6	5	318	3.5	47.5
Malaysia	7	7	269	2.9	50.5
Australia	8	11	255	2.8	53.2
India	9	9	232	2.5	55.7
Singapore	10	8	216	2.3	58.1
Brazil	11	12	213	2.3	60.4
Russian Federation	12	17	201	2.2	62.6
Viet Nam	13	20	187	2.0	64.6
Thailand	14	10	185	2.0	66.6
United Arab Emirates	15	16	184	2.0	68.6
Rest of the world			2 895	31.4	100.0
World			**9 220**	**100.0**	–

1.3 Trade structure by product

Map 1.3 Main export products, 2021

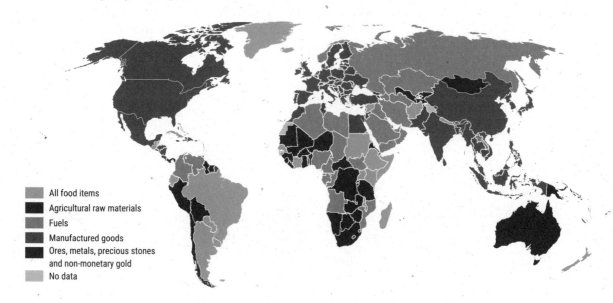

All food items
Agricultural raw materials
Fuels
Manufactured goods
Ores, metals, precious stones
and non-monetary gold
No data

Concepts and definitions

The breakdown of merchandise trade by product group is based on the entries in the customs declarations that are coded in accordance with a globally harmonized classification system, called the Harmonized Commodity Description and Coding System (HS). The values of the individual customs declarations have been summed up to the level of product group, error-checked and submitted to the United Nations Statistics Division for integration in the UN Comtrade database (United Nations, 2022).

The UN Comtrade database contains product breakdowns based on the Standard International Trade Classification (SITC). These have been obtained by conversion of the raw data coded in HS and constitute the main source of the figures presented in this section. For correspondence between SITC codes and the five broad product groups presented in this section, see annex 6.2.

Regional specialization patterns

The supply of goods to the world market has a regional pattern. In 2021, economies in Northern and Central America, Europe and Southern, Eastern and South-Eastern Asia exported mainly manufactured goods. Economies mainly exporting fuels were located along the northern coast of South America, in Middle and Northern Africa and Western and Central Asia.

In Africa, primary goods accounted for 77 per cent of merchandise exports in 2021. Fuels made up 44 per cent. Developing Asia and Oceania relied much less on primary goods exports (24 per cent) than developing economies in Africa and the Americas. Among the three developing regions, developing America recorded the largest proportion of food exports (24 per cent), and developing Asia and Oceania the lowest (5 per cent).

Figure 1.3.1 Export structure of developing economies by product group, 2021
(Percentage)

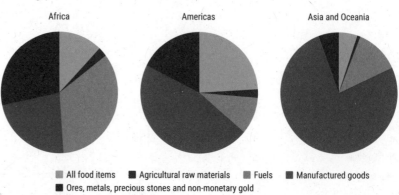

Africa   Americas   Asia and Oceania

All food items   Agricultural raw materials   Fuels   Manufactured goods
Ores, metals, precious stones and non-monetary gold

Note: Non-allocated products are not considered.

Trade rebound in all product groups

The global rebound of merchandise trade in 2021 (see section 1.1) was intensely driven by the surge in fuels trade. Fuels exports increased sharply, by 72 per cent. Exports of ores, metals, precious stones, and non-monetary gold grew by 34 per cent and exports of agricultural raw materials increased by 32 per cent. Exports of food grew by 18 per cent, just behind the 22 per cent growth of manufactured goods.

Figure 1.3.2 Annual growth rate of exports by product group, 2021
(Percentage)

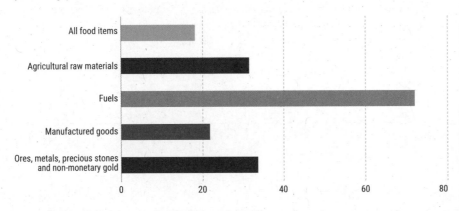

What do developing regions trade with others?

In 2021, developing economies in Asia and Oceania recorded a merchandise trade surplus of 10 per cent driven by high exports of manufactured goods. Africa's high imports of manufactured products were only partly offset by surpluses in fuel and in ores, metals, precious stones, and monetary gold. Overall, a nine per cent trade deficit remained. In developing economies of the Americas, positive trade balances in food, in agricultural raw materials, and in ores, metals, precious stones, and monetary gold were not enough to offset a negative trade balance in manufacturing. Five per cent trade deficit persisted.

Figure 1.3.3 Developing economies' extra-trade structure, 2021
(Percentage of exports)

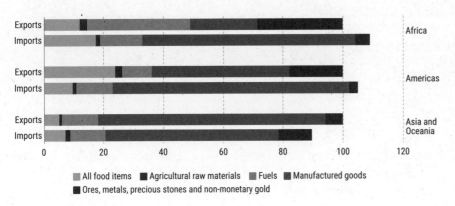

Note: Non-allocated products are not considered.

Manufactures exporters
mostly found in

Northern and Central America   Europe   South and East Asia

77% of Africa's merchandise **exports** are **primary goods**

World **fuels** trade grew **by 72%** in 2021

In 2021 **Africa imported 3 times more manufactured** goods than it exported

Table 1.3 | **Exports by product group, origin and destination, 2021**
(Millions of United States dollars)

All food items

Origin	Destination					
				Developing economies		
	World	Developed economies	Total	Africa	Americas	Asia and Oceania
World	**1 885 346**	**1 105 648**	**777 492**	**103 195**	**108 712**	**565 585**
	(100)	(59)	(41)	(5)	(6)	(30)
Developed economies	1 126 352	794 348	330 293	43 534	58 958	227 801
	(100)	(71)	(29)	(4)	(5)	(20)
Developing economies	758 994	311 300	447 199	59 662	49 753	337 784
	(100)	(41)	(59)	(8)	(7)	(45)
Developing economies: Africa	67 389	32 943	34 333	15 803	547	17 983
	(100)	(49)	(51)	(23)	(1)	(27)
Developing economies: Americas	274 823	130 751	143 773	11 808	42 184	89 781
	(100)	(48)	(52)	(4)	(15)	(33)
Developing economies: Asia and Oceania	416 783	147 606	269 094	32 051	7 022	230 020
	(100)	(35)	(65)	(8)	(2)	(55)

Note: Percentage of exports to the whole world in parentheses.

Agricultural raw materials

Origin	Destination					
				Developing economies		
	World	Developed economies	Total	Africa	Americas	Asia and Oceania
World	**305 701**	**162 378**	**142 484**	**7 874**	**11 787**	**122 824**
	(100)	(53)	(47)	(3)	(4)	(40)
Developed economies	198 206	125 661	71 783	4 778	7 898	59 107
	(100)	(63)	(36)	(2)	(4)	(30)
Developing economies	107 495	36 717	70 702	3 096	3 889	63 717
	(100)	(34)	(66)	(3)	(4)	(59)
Developing economies: Africa	14 154	4 321	9 832	972	103	8 756
	(100)	(31)	(69)	(7)	(1)	(62)
Developing economies: Americas	25 703	11 612	14 016	184	2 078	11 754
	(100)	(45)	(55)	(1)	(8)	(46)
Developing economies: Asia and Oceania	67 638	20 783	46 854	1 940	1 707	43 207
	(100)	(31)	(69)	(3)	(3)	(64)

Note: Percentage of exports to the whole world in parentheses.

Fuels

Origin	Destination					
	World	Developed economies	Developing economies			
			Total	Africa	Americas	Asia and Oceania
World	**2 558 349**	**1 307 033**	**1 158 043**	**91 587**	**140 760**	**925 696**
	(100)	(51)	(45)	(4)	(6)	(36)
Developed economies	1 260 976	832 455	356 178	34 293	103 236	218 649
	(100)	(66)	(28)	(3)	(8)	(17)
Developing economies	1 297 373	474 578	801 865	57 294	37 524	707 047
	(100)	(37)	(62)	(4)	(3)	(54)
Developing economies: Africa	191 509	93 191	97 666	13 836	4 524	79 305
	(100)	(49)	(51)	(7)	(2)	(41)
Developing economies: Americas	113 469	31 621	64 593	965	23 618	40 010
	(100)	(28)	(57)	(1)	(21)	(35)
Developing economies: Asia and Oceania	992 395	349 766	639 605	42 492	9 382	587 731
	(100)	(35)	(64)	(4)	(1)	(59)

Note: Percentage of exports to the whole world in parentheses.

Manufactured goods

Origin	Destination					
	World	Developed economies	Developing economies			
			Total	Africa	Americas	Asia and Oceania
World	**15 089 007**	**9 274 113**	**5 804 372**	**427 705**	**862 657**	**4 514 011**
	(100)	(61)	(38)	(3)	(6)	(30)
Developed economies	8 244 978	5 948 366	2 288 374	160 676	472 175	1 655 523
	(100)	(72)	(28)	(2)	(6)	(20)
Developing economies	6 844 029	3 325 747	3 515 999	267 029	390 482	2 858 488
	(100)	(49)	(51)	(4)	(6)	(42)
Developing economies: Africa	126 863	68 118	57 847	27 510	6 135	24 202
	(100)	(54)	(46)	(22)	(5)	(19)
Developing economies: Americas	527 791	422 955	103 761	2 699	84 736	16 327
	(100)	(80)	(20)	(1)	(16)	(3)
Developing economies: Asia and Oceania	6 189 375	2 834 673	3 354 390	236 819	299 612	2 817 959
	(100)	(46)	(54)	(4)	(5)	(46)

Note: Percentage of exports to the whole world in parentheses.

Ores, metals, precious stones and non-monetary gold

Origin	Destination					
	World	Developed economies	Developing economies			
			Total	Africa	Americas	Asia and Oceania
World	**1 725 949**	**824 344**	**888 318**	**32 443**	**33 428**	**822 447**
	(100)	(48)	(51)	(2)	(2)	(48)
Developed economies	911 705	530 553	368 454	8 755	16 946	342 753
	(100)	(58)	(40)	(1)	(2)	(38)
Developing economies	814 244	293 791	519 864	23 688	16 481	479 695
	(100)	(36)	(64)	(3)	(2)	(59)
Developing economies: Africa	158 461	57 821	100 628	12 620	954	87 054
	(100)	(36)	(64)	(8)	(1)	(55)
Developing economies: Americas	201 082	83 581	116 933	812	8 726	107 396
	(100)	(42)	(58)	(0)	(4)	(53)
Developing economies: Asia and Oceania	454 701	152 389	302 303	10 257	6 802	285 244
	(100)	(34)	(66)	(2)	(1)	(63)

Note: Percentage of exports to the whole world in parentheses.

1.4 Trade indicators

Map 1.4 Trade openness index, 2021
(Percentage)

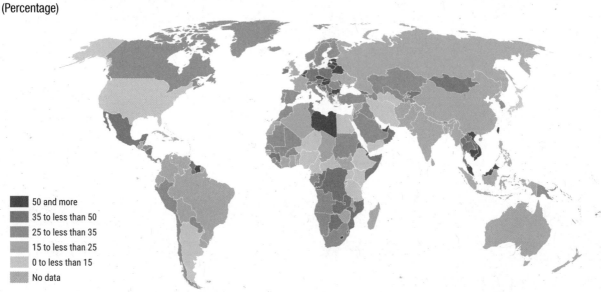

- 50 and more
- 35 to less than 50
- 25 to less than 35
- 15 to less than 25
- 0 to less than 15
- No data

Note: This index measures the importance of international trade in goods relative to the domestic economic output of an economy. Exports are given equal weight to imports.

Concepts and definitions

This section presents different indices that can be used to analyze trade flows and trade patterns over time from the perspective of, for example, relative competitiveness, structure of global exports and imports markets, or the importance of trade for the economy, both for individual economies and for groups of economies.

For information on how the indices in this section are calculated, see annex 6.3. The presented indices are a subset of the trade indices available at UNCTADstat (UNCTAD, 2022a).

How important is trade for economies?

In 2021, Hong Kong SAR remained the most open economy to international trade, as indicated by the trade openness index of 182 per cent. Singapore (115 per cent), Viet Nam (115 cent), and Djibouti (100 per cent) ranked second, third and fourth. The index stood at 17 and 16 per cent respectively in China and India. Japan and the United States of America recorded an index score of 15 per cent or below. Iran is identified as the least open economy (5 per cent).

How did the relative price of exports to imports develop?

In 2021, the terms of trade improved in almost all geographical regions, except Asia, where they declined by 0.6 per cent. The largest increase of 23.3 per cent was recorded in Oceania, followed by Africa (22.3 per cent) and Northern America (7.1 per cent). The terms of trade of European countries was 1.6 per cent higher than in the previous year.

Figure 1.4.1 Terms of trade index
(2015=100)

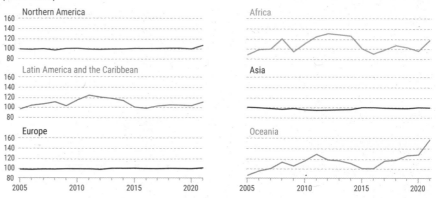

Note: This index indicates how much the relative price between exports and imports has changed in relation to the base year.

How concentrated is global product supply?

Large differences persist in the degree to which global supply is concentrated among exporting economies. Over the past 17 years, manufactured products have been the product group with the highest concentration of exports supply among economies with the index score averaging 0.19 for the period. In 2021, it stood at 0.21, as compared to index scores between 0.12 and 0.15 recorded for the other product groups. Fuels (0.15) remained the group with the second highest market concentration of exports.

Figure 1.4.2 Market concentration index of exports

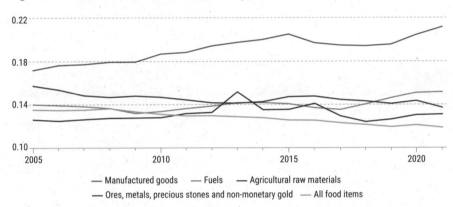

— Manufactured goods   — Fuels   — Agricultural raw materials
— Ores, metals, precious stones and non-monetary gold   — All food items

Note: This index measures the extent to which a high proportion of exports is delivered by a small number of economies. It has a value of 1 if all exports originate from a single economy.

How concentrated was the structure of exports?

Export diversification varies significantly across regions. In 2021, the highest concentration of exports over products was recorded by Western Asia and Northern Africa (0.28), followed by Oceania (0.27) and Sub-Saharan Africa (0.22). Exports of European (0.06) and Northern American (0.08) economies were more diversified. Five African countries with strong reliance on exports of natural resources had the world's highest product concentration of exports: the South Sudan (0.93), Botswana (0.89), Mali (0.89), Guinea-Bissau (0.88), and Chad (0.87).

Figure 1.4.3 Product concentration index of exports, 2021

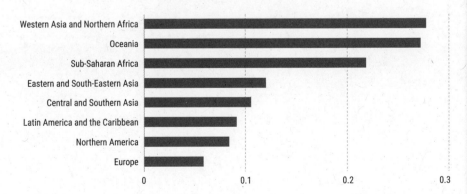

Note: This index measures the extent to which a large share of exports is accounted for by a small number of product groups. The index has a value of 1 when an economy exports only one group of products and a value of 0 if all product groups are equally represented.

Hong Kong SAR ranks **highest** in trade-openness

Iran is placed at the **bottom**

Oceania's terms of trade improved in 2021

+23.3%

Global supply of manufactured goods more concentrated than other product groups among exporters

Exports from **Western Asia and Northern Africa** highly concentrated on a **narrow range of products**

Table 1.4.1 | **Selected trade indices by group of economies**
(2015=100)

Developed economies

Year	Volume[a]		Purchasing power of exports[b]	Terms of trade[c]
	Imports	Exports		
2011	93	92	88	96
2019	111	108	107	99
2020	106	102	103	100
2021	115	111	112	101

[a] This index indicates the change in exports or imports, adjusted for the movement of prices, relative to the base year.
[b] This index indicates the change in exports, valued in prices of imports, relative to the base year.
[c] See note, figure 1.4.1 above.

Developing economies

Year	Volume[a]		Purchasing power of exports[b]	Terms of trade[c]
	Imports	Exports		
2011	87	91	91	100
2019	111	111	111	100
2020	106	109	109	101
2021	119	119	123	103

Developing economies: Africa

Year	Volume[a]		Purchasing power of exports[b]	Terms of trade[c]
	Imports	Exports		
2011	81	106	123	116
2019	99	106	116	109
2020	85	93	97	104
2021	91	93	116	124

[a] This index indicates the change in exports or imports, adjusted for the movement of prices, relative to the base year.
[b] This index indicates the change in exports, valued in prices of imports, relative to the base year.
[c] See note, figure 1.4.1 above.

Developing economies: Americas

Year	Volume[a]		Purchasing power of exports[b]	Terms of trade[c]
	Imports	Exports		
2011	97	89	110	124
2019	104	108	112	104
2020	90	102	106	104
2021	111	108	119	111

Developing economies: Asia and Oceania

Year	Volume[a]		Purchasing power of exports[b]	Terms of trade[c]
	Imports	Exports		
2011	86	89	85	96
2019	113	113	111	98
2020	111	111	111	100
2021	124	124	124	100

[a] This index indicates the change in exports or imports, adjusted for the movement of prices, relative to the base year.
[b] This index indicates the change in exports, valued in prices of imports, relative to the base year.
[c] See note, figure 1.4.1 above.

Table 1.4.2 | **Selected trade indices, landlocked developing countries**
(2015=100)

Economy	Volume[a] Imports		Volume[a] Exports		Purchasing power of exports[b]		Terms of trade[c]	
	2020	2021	2020	2021	2020	2021	2020	2021
Afghanistan	82	55	112	130	132	137	118	106
Armenia	144	122	147	138	175	150	120	108
Azerbaijan	109	109	97	73	78	115	80	157
Bhutan	80	93	107	76	112	116	105	151
Bolivia (Plurinational State of)	62	75	70	74	69	97	98	131
Botswana	90	102	70	117	66	101	94	86
Burkina Faso	130	116	137	148	195	179	142	121
Burundi	102	103	110	94	129	111	117	117
Central African Republic	165	147	152	176	149	163	98	93
Chad	67	64	92	77	74	92	80	119
Eswatini	109	117	95	92	93	97	98	106
Ethiopia	76	79	110	107	109	112	99	105
Kazakhstan	114	104	103	76	95	102	92	133
Kyrgyzstan	89	116	102	78	133	97	131	125
Lao People's Dem. Rep.	90	89	144	99	160	169	111	170
Lesotho	85	78	97	112	90	87	93	78
Malawi	115	123	76	90	70	81	93	90
Mali	133	139	120	120	175	149	146	124
Moldova, Republic of	139	161	114	132	128	143	113	108
Mongolia	135	148	126	110	157	162	125	148
Nepal	141	187	110	172	113	183	102	107
Niger	111	111	95	84	94	89	99	105
North Macedonia	126	133	141	154	136	135	96	88
Paraguay	110	134	90	88	113	128	125	146
Rwanda	97	98	159	151	188	181	119	119
Tajikistan	88	96	119	139	151	189	127	136
Turkmenistan	44	50	113	44	62	80	55	185
Uganda	134	121	157	131	164	141	104	108
Uzbekistan	166	177	123	78	132	128	108	164
Zambia	61	70	107	107	109	131	102	122
Zimbabwe	78	88	116	141	127	138	109	98

[a] This index indicates the change in exports or imports, adjusted for the movement of prices, relative to the base year.
[b] This index indicates the change in exports, valued in prices of imports, relative to the base year.
[c] See note, figure 1.4.1 above.

2

INTERNATIONAL TRADE IN SERVICES

KEY FIGURES **2021**

Value of world
services exports
US$**6.1** trillion

Change of world
services exports
+17.2%

Share of travel in
world services
exports
10.1%

NOWCAST **2022**

Growth of global
services exports
+14.6%

2.1 Total trade in services

Map 2.1 Exports of services as a ratio to gross domestic product, 2021
(Percentage)

- 20 and more
- 10 to less than 20
- 3 to less than 10
- 0 to less than 3
- No data

Concepts and definitions

In this chapter, in accordance with the concepts of the balance of payments (IMF, 2009) and national accounts (United Nations et al., 2009), services are understood as the result of a production activity that changes the conditions of the consuming units, or facilitates the exchange of products or financial assets.

International trade in services takes place when a service is supplied in any of the following modes: from one economy to another (services cross the border); within an economy to service a consumer of another economy (consumer crosses the border); or through the presence of natural persons of one economy in another economy (supplier crosses the border) (United Nations et al., 2012).

Trade-in-services figures are jointly compiled by UNCTAD and WTO.

Recovery in 2021, solid growth in 2022

After the pandemic-driven decline of 17.7 per cent in 2020, world services exports entered a recovery path in 2021. Growth in services exports of 14.6 per cent is nowcast for 2022. This would mean a new record high of US$7 trillion.

In 2021, global services exports were valued at US$6.1 trillion, representing 6.3 per cent of world GDP and 21.4 per cent of total world trade in both goods and services. After the plunge of travel and transport during the pandemic in 2020, international services flows recovered in 2021 and almost reached their 2019 levels.

In 2021, the services exports' share in GDP exceeded 30 per cent in 22 economies. Those are either small islands where travel exports are important, or other small economies with significant business and financial services exports. Notably, Luxembourg and Malta recorded services exports at 165 and 110 per cent of GDP, respectively.

Figure 2.1.1 World services exports
(Trillions of United States dollars)

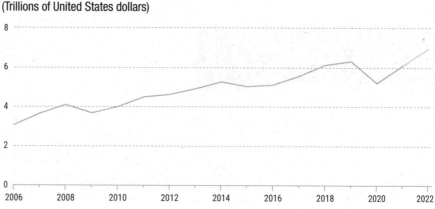

Note: The dotted line indicates UNCTAD nowcasts. For the weekly update of the nowcast and its methodology, see UNCTAD (2022b).

All regions recovered in 2021

Looking at the trends by development status and region, a solid recovery of services exports was observed in all groups of economies. The highest relative rise was measured in American developing economies, where travel and transport have held a prominent role and had more ground to recover after the pandemic. Asian developing economies' growth was less driven by recovery in travel, but rather by a significant rise in transport exports, as well as in intellectual property, insurance, and business services that those economies supplied abroad.

Figure 2.1.2 Services trade annual growth rates, 2021
(Percentage)

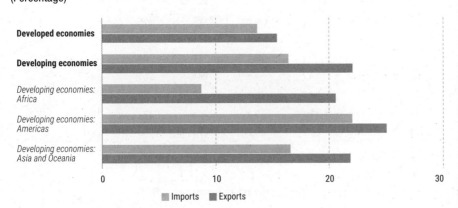

Leading services exporters

With US$795 billion worth of services sold internationally in 2021, the United States of America remained the world's leading exporter, capturing a 13 per cent share of the global market. It was followed, at some distance, by the United Kingdom (US$418 billion). China, the leading exporter among developing economies, ranked third (US$392 billion). The top five services exporters from the developing world were Asian. In 2021, they captured 17 per cent of the global market.

Figure 2.1.3 Top five services exporters, 2021
(Billions of United States dollars)

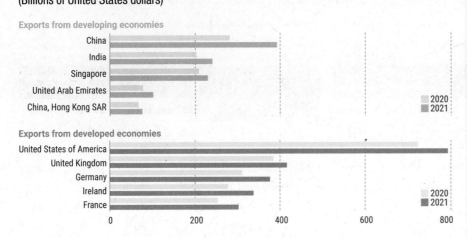

Global services exports nowcast to reach US$7 trillion in 2022

International services exports accounted for 6.3% of world GDP in 2021

6.3%

almost 1 percentage point less than before COVID-19

In 2021, developing economies' services exports recovered well by 22% from 2020

Top 5 exporters from the developing world

supplied 17%

of internationally traded services in 2021

Table 2.1.1 | **Trade in services by group of economies**

Group of economies	Exports				Imports			
	Value		Share in world	Biannual change[a]	Value		Share in world	Biannual change[a]
	(Billions of US$)		(Percentage)	(Percentage)	(Billions of US$)		(Percentage)	(Percentage)
	2019	2021	2021	2019–2021	2019	2021	2021	2019–2021
World	**6 291**	**6 072**	**100.0**	**-3.5**	**6 033**	**5 623**	**100.0**	**-6.8**
Developed economies	4 505	4 421	72.8	-1.9	3 971	3 768	67.0	-5.1
Developing economies	1 786	1 651	27.2	-7.6	2 062	1 855	33.0	-10.0
Developing economies: Africa	126	100	1.7	-20.3	191	160	2.8	-16.4
Developing economies: Americas	201	158	2.6	-21.8	229	198	3.5	-13.6
Developing economies: Asia and Oceania	1 458	1 393	22.9	-4.5	1 642	1 498	26.6	-8.8
Selected groups								
Developing economies excluding China	1 503	1 259	20.7	-16.2	1 561	1 414	25.1	-9.4
Developing economies excluding LDCs	1 737	1 616	26.6	-6.9	1 990	1 784	31.7	-10.3
LDCs	49	35	0.6	-29.7	71	71	1.3	-0.5
LLDCs	46	36	0.6	-22.3	71	64	1.1	-10.5
SIDS (UN-OHRLLS)	288	287	4.7	-0.6	247	265	4.7	7.0
HIPCs (IMF)	43	36	0.6	-16.0	67	70	1.2	3.4
BRICS	611	732	12.1	19.8	865	777	13.8	-10.2
G20	4 913	4 901	80.7	-0.2	4 670	4 386	78.0	-6.1

[a] Year 2021 compared to pre-pandemic year 2019, percentage difference.

Table 2.1.2 | **Leading services exporters and importers by group of economies, 2021**

Developed economies

Exporter (Ranked by value)	Value	Share in world total	Annual growth rate	Importer (Ranked by value)	Value	Share in world total	Annual growth rate
	(Billions of US$)	(Percentage)	(Percentage)		(Billions of US$)	(Percentage)	(Percentage)
United States of America	795	13.1	9.5	United States of America	550	9.8	17.9
United Kingdom	418	6.9	8.2	Germany	(e) 381	(e) 6.8	(e) 22.5
Germany	(e) 377	(e) 6.2	(e) 21.4	Ireland	341	6.1	-2.3
Ireland	338	5.6	21.2	France	258	4.6	9.5
France	303	5.0	19.0	United Kingdom	243	4.3	14.7
Developed economies	**4 421**	**72.8**	**15.5**	**Developed economies**	**3 768**	**67.0**	**13.7**

Developing economies

Exporter (Ranked by value)	Value	Share in world total	Annual growth rate	Importer (Ranked by value)	Value	Share in world total	Annual growth rate
	(Billions of US$)	(Percentage)	(Percentage)		(Billions of US$)	(Percentage)	(Percentage)
China	(e) 392	(e) 6.5	(e) 39.8	China	(e) 441	(e) 7.8	(e) 15.8
India	241	4.0	18.5	Singapore	224	4.0	9.7
Singapore	230	3.8	9.6	India	(e) 196	(e) 3.5	(e) 27.5
United Arab Emirates	102	1.7	30.4	United Arab Emirates	76	1.4	23.0
China, Hong Kong SAR	77	1.3	14.7	Saudi Arabia	73	1.3	30.2
Developing economies	**1 651**	**27.2**	**22.1**	**Developing economies**	**1 855**	**33.0**	**16.4**

Developing economies: Africa

Exporter (Ranked by value)	Value (Billions of US$)	Share in world total (Percentage)	Annual growth rate (Percentage)
Egypt	(e) 22	(e) 0.4	(e) 45.5
Morocco	15	0.3	11.5
Ghana	(e) 9	(e) 0.2	(e) 20.6
South Africa	9	0.1	5.2
Ethiopia	(e) 6	(e) 0.1	(e) 25.0
Developing Africa	**100**	**1.7**	**20.6**

Importer (Ranked by value)	Value (Billions of US$)	Share in world total (Percentage)	Annual growth rate (Percentage)
Egypt	(e) 23	(e) 0.4	(e) 26.1
Nigeria	(e) 15	(e) 0.3	(e) -23.5
South Africa	14	0.2	20.1
Ghana	(e) 12	(e) 0.2	(e) 1.8
Morocco	9	0.2	19.4
Developing Africa	**160**	**2.8**	**8.8**

Developing economies: Americas

Exporter (Ranked by value)	Value (Billions of US$)	Share in world total (Percentage)	Annual growth rate (Percentage)
Brazil	33	0.5	16.1
Mexico	(e) 27	(e) 0.4	(e) 60.4
Panama	11	0.2	25.4
Argentina	9	0.2	-0.4
Costa Rica	(e) 9	(e) 0.1	(e) 12.3
Developing Americas	**158**	**2.6**	**25.1**

Importer (Ranked by value)	Value (Billions of US$)	Share in world total (Percentage)	Annual growth rate (Percentage)
Brazil	50	0.9	1.5
Mexico	(e) 39	(e) 0.7	(e) 37.7
Chile	(e) 16	(e) 0.3	(e) 39.3
Colombia	(e) 13	(e) 0.2	(e) 30.1
Argentina	13	0.2	10.3
Developing Americas	**198**	**3.5**	**22.1**

Developing economies: Asia and Oceania

Exporter (Ranked by value)	Value (Billions of US$)	Share in world total (Percentage)	Annual growth rate (Percentage)
China	(e) 392	(e) 6.5	(e) 39.8
India	241	4.0	18.5
Singapore	230	3.8	9.6
United Arab Emirates	102	1.7	30.4
China, Hong Kong SAR	77	1.3	14.7
Developing Asia and Oceania	**1 393**	**22.9**	**21.9**

Importer (Ranked by value)	Value (Billions of US$)	Share in world total (Percentage)	Annual growth rate (Percentage)
China	(e) 441	(e) 7.8	(e) 15.8
Singapore	224	4.0	9.7
India	(e) 196	(e) 3.5	(e) 27.5
United Arab Emirates	76	1.4	23.0
Saudi Arabia	73	1.3	30.2
Developing Asia and Oceania	**1 498**	**26.6**	**16.6**

2.2 Trade in services by category

Map 2.2 Growth in services exports by category, 2016–2021
(Average annual growth rate*, percentage)

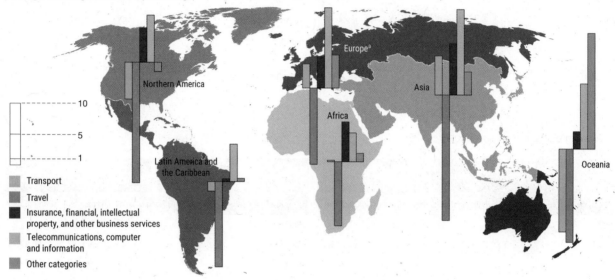

* Least squares growth rate (see annex 6.3).
a Including the Russian Federation and the French overseas departments.

Concepts and definitions

The breakdown by service category in this section has been built from the division of services in the balance of payments statistics, known as the 2010 Extended Balance of Payments Services Classification (EBOPS 2010) (United Nations et al., 2012). For the correspondence to the EBOPS 2010 categories and to the main groups presented in UNCTADstat, see annex 6.2.

The presented trade-in-services figures are jointly compiled by UNCTAD and WTO.

Regional trends over the last five years

International trade in services was more severely hit by the COVID-19 pandemic than merchandise trade. Among services, travel and transport were most affected. Owing to a renewed demand for goods, transport recovered rapidly and strongly in 2021, especially in Asia and Europe. By contrast, travel, particularly long-distance travel, continued to suffer, pinning the five-year average growth rate of global international travel receipts to -16 per cent.

From 2016 to 2019, services trade enjoyed growth across main services categories on all continents. Africa's travel exports rose substantially, while other regions registered solid gains in telecommunications and computer services. Financial, insurance, business, and intellectual property services rose globally before and then remained afloat during the pandemic. Expectedly, telecommunications and computer services' exports grew during the pandemic, especially in Europe and Asia.

Figure 2.2.1 Annual growth rate of services exports, 2021
(Percentage)

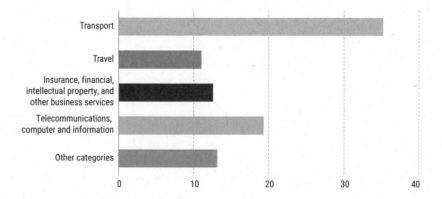

Global trends by service category in 2021

Among main service categories, transport exports recorded the highest annual growth in 2021 (+35 per cent). They were followed by exports of telecommunications, computer, and information services, which rose by 19 per cent. After plummeting by over 60 per cent in 2020, travel recovered just partially during 2021, rising by 11 per cent. This sector remained particularly significant in services trade of Africa and developing America. Transport and travel together accounted for over half of their services exports. In developed economies, travel and transport represented one quarter of total services sold abroad.

Figure 2.2.2 Structure of services exports, 2021

(Percentage)

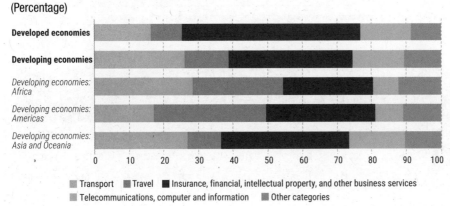

Transport **services exports**
↑35% up **in 2021 –**
more than a
recovery from
the pandemic

Telecommunications, computer, and information services

In 2021, 73 per cent of global services were supplied from developed economies, whose exports were dominated by insurance, financial, intellectual property, telecommunications, computer, and other business services. Telecommunications, computer, and information services continued to build on the strong demand during the pandemic. Globally, they expanded by 19 per cent in 2021, more than double their growth from the year before. African exports of those services were 14 per cent higher in 2021 than in 2020. With 20 per cent growth, American developing economies caught up with the increasing trend in other regions for this service category. These services often underpin intra-firm collaboration, business-to-business and business-to-clients connectivity, and digital trade.

International
travel struggled
to regain ground
in 2021

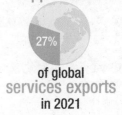

Developing **economies**
supplied 27%

27%

of global
services exports
in 2021

Figure 2.2.3 Growth of exports of telecommunications, computer, and information services, by group of economies, 2019–2021

(Percentage)

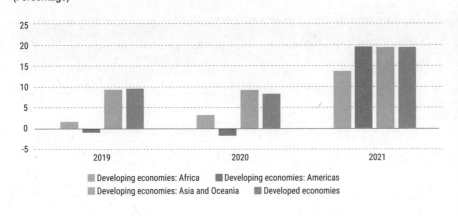

Solid growth of IT
services exports
in African **and**
American developing
economies

Table 2.2.1 | **Trade in services by service category and group of economies**

World

Service category	Exports Value (Billions of US$)		Exports Annual growth rate (Percentage)	Imports Value (Billions of US$)		Imports Annual growth rate (Percentage)
	2016	2021	2021	2016	2021	2021
Total services	**5 091**	**6 072**	**17.2**	**4 930**	**5 623**	**14.6**
Transport	861	1 158	35.3	1 018	1 374	34.0
Travel	1 234	615	11.1	1 212	610	9.4
Others	2 996	4 298	14.0	2 701	3 639	9.4

Note: Exports do not equal imports at world level, due to imperfect geographical coverage and cross-country differences in compilation methods.

Developed economies

Service category	Exports Value (Billions of US$)		Exports Annual growth rate (Percentage)	Imports Value (Billions of US$)		Imports Annual growth rate (Percentage)	Balance (Billions of US$)	
	2016	2021	2021	2016	2021	2021	2016	2021
Total services	**3 694**	**4 421**	**15.5**	**3 182**	**3 768**	**13.7**	**512**	**653**
Transport	579	726	30.2	563	718	31.8	16	8
Travel	760	404	10.8	644	345	21.2	116	59
Others	2 355	3 290	13.2	1 975	2 705	8.9	380	585

Developing economies

Service category	Exports Value (Billions of US$)		Exports Annual growth rate (Percentage)	Imports Value (Billions of US$)		Imports Annual growth rate (Percentage)	Balance (Billions of US$)	
	2016	2021	2021	2016	2021	2021	2016	2021
Total services	**1 397**	**1 651**	**22.1**	**1 748**	**1 855**	**16.4**	**-352**	**-204**
Transport	282	432	44.7	455	656	36.6	-173	-224
Travel	473	211	11.5	568	265	-2.8	-95	-54
Others	641	1 008	16.6	726	934	11.2	-84	74

Developing economies: Africa

Service category	Exports Value (Billions of US$)		Exports Annual growth rate (Percentage)	Imports Value (Billions of US$)		Imports Annual growth rate (Percentage)	Balance (Billions of US$)	
	2016	2021	2021	2016	2021	2021	2016	2021
Total services	**95**	**100**	**20.6**	**142**	**160**	**8.8**	**-47**	**-59**
Transport	26	29	16.0	55	64	18.7	-28	-36
Travel	35	26	33.9	20	19	10.2	14	7
Others	34	46	17.0	66	76	1.3	-32	-31

Developing economies: Americas

Service category	Exports			Imports			Balance	
	Value		Annual growth rate	Value		Annual growth rate		
	(Billions of US$)		(Percentage)	(Billions of US$)		(Percentage)	(Billions of US$)	
	2016	2021	2021	2016	2021	2021	2016	2021
Total services	**179**	**158**	**25.1**	**210**	**198**	**22.1**	**-31**	**-40**
Transport	26	27	22.4	55	73	58.4	-28	-45
Travel	83	51	46.7	55	22	23.1	29	29
Others	69	79	15.1	100	103	4.9	-31	-23

Developing economies: Asia and Oceania

Service category	Exports			Imports			Balance	
	Value		Annual growth rate	Value		Annual growth rate		
	(Billions of US$)		(Percentage)	(Billions of US$)		(Percentage)	(Billions of US$)	
	2016	2021	2021	2016	2021	2021	2016	2021
Total services	**1 123**	**1 393**	**21.9**	**1 397**	**1 498**	**16.6**	**-274**	**-105**
Transport	229	377	49.5	345	519	36.5	-116	-143
Travel	355	133	-0.9	493	223	-5.8	-137	-90
Others	538	883	16.8	559	755	13.2	-21	128

Table 2.2.2 | **Exports of selected services, by region, 2021**
(Millions of United States dollars)

Group of economies	Insurance and pension services	Financial services	Charges for the use of intellectual property n.i.e.	Telecommunications, computer, and information services	Other business services
World	**183 262**	**630 319**	**452 082**	**896 418**	**1 595 661**
Northern America	24 459	183 471	133 149	72 889	254 069
Latin America and the Caribbean	6 593	5 812	1 263	12 865	36 019
Europe	97 582	330 189	223 462	525 374	827 053
Sub-Saharan Africa	1 028	3 985	299	3 667	13 048
Western Asia and Northern Africa	32 154	5 579	7 557	48 514	41 608
Central and Southern Asia	3 370	5 813	949	87 128	97 510
Eastern and South-Eastern Asia	17 414	91 692	83 028	140 385	315 900
Oceania	663	3 778	2 375	5 595	10 454
Selected groups					
Developing economies excluding China	52 132	87 565	23 598	168 437	311 369
Developing economies excluding LDCs	57 228	92 073	35 492	243 124	401 044
LDCs	210	599	54	2 305	3 942
LLDCs	357	597	106	2 866	4 107
SIDS (UN-OHRLLS)	14 846	39 664	11 705	21 744	81 334
HIPCs (IMF)	400	1 446	92	2 091	9 019
BRICS	9 912	13 822	15 094	170 336	218 262
G20	132 740	523 132	396 928	765 620	1 338 244

3

ECONOMIC TRENDS

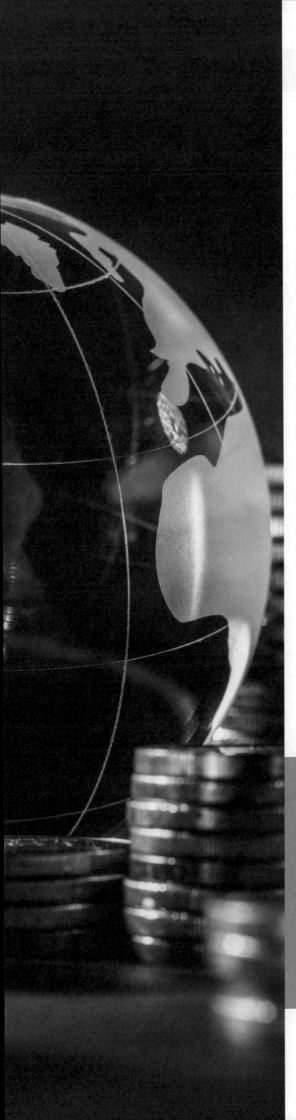

KEY FIGURES **2021**

Change of world real
GDP per capita

+4.7%

FDI inflows to LDCs

US$26 billion

UNCTAD Commodity
Price Index

+55%

NOWCAST **2022**

World real GDP
growth

+3.3%

3.1 Gross domestic product

Map 3.1 Gross domestic product per capita, 2021
(United States dollars)

- 30 000 and more
- 8 000 to less than 30 000
- 3 000 to less than 8 000
- 1 000 to less than 3 000
- 0 to less than 1 000
- No data

Concepts and definitions

GDP is an aggregate measure of production, income and expenditure of an economy. As a production measure, it represents the gross value added, i.e., the output net of intermediate consumption, achieved by all resident units engaged in production, plus any taxes less subsidies on products not included in the value of output. As an income measure, it represents the sum of primary incomes (gross wages and entrepreneurial income) distributed by resident producers, plus taxes less subsidies on production and imports. As an expenditure measure, it depicts the sum of expenditure on final consumption, gross capital formation (i.e., investment, changes in inventories, and acquisitions less disposals of valuables) and exports after deduction of imports (United Nations et al., 2009).

The GDP figures presented in this section are usually calculated from the expenditure side.

Trends in global economy

After a sharp contraction of 3.4 per cent in 2020, the world's real GDP expanded by 5.7 per cent in 2021, the fastest annual growth since 1973. In 2022, GDP growth is nowcast to slow down to 3.3 per cent.

Large differences in GDP per capita persist throughout the world. In 2021, most developed economies produced an output per person greater than US$30 000, with economies in Eastern and Northern Europe as the main exceptions. By contrast, almost half of the developing economies in Africa – all of them least developed countries (LDCs) – recorded a per capita output of less than US$1 300. Most developing economies in the Americas, Asia and Oceania reached an output higher than US$3 000 per person.

Figure 3.1.1 World real gross domestic product, annual growth rate
(Percentage)

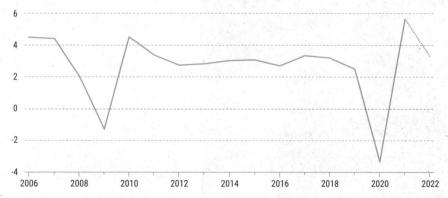

Note: In constant 2015 United States dollars. The dotted line indicates UNCTAD nowcasts. For the weekly update of the nowcast and its methodology, see UNCTAD (2022b).

Regional trends

Growth was unevenly distributed across regions in 2021. Developed regions bounced back from the COVID-19 pandemic with a growth rate of 5.0 per cent. After a strong contraction of 2.7 per cent in 2020, developing Africa's GDP expanded by 5.0 per cent in 2021. Developing Asia's GDP growth rebounded from -0.4 per cent to 7.0 per cent in 2021. Developing Americas' GDP increased by 6.2 per cent in 2021, following a 7.4 per cent drop in 2020.

LDCs' GDP grew by 2.0 per cent in 2021 remaining below the 7 per cent target set by the 2030 Agenda for Sustainable Development. At the same time, their GDP per capita declined by 0.4 per cent.

Figure 3.1.2 Growth of real gross domestic product by group of economies, 2021
(Percentage)

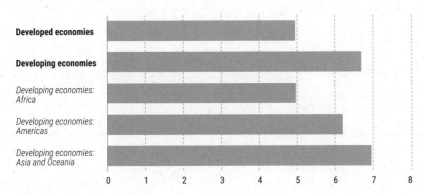

Note: In constant 2015 United States dollars.

Global economic inequality

Over the last 10 years, the global distribution of nominal GDP across economies has trended towards more equal. For example, in 2011, the poorest economies, accounting for 85 per cent of the world's population, contributed 36 per cent to world GDP. By 2021, their share in GDP was 40 per cent. The last five years, however, did not show any clear reduction in inequality.

The highest GDP per capita, in nominal terms, was recorded for Luxembourg (US$132 918), Bermuda (US$126 972), Cayman Islands (US$99 007), Ireland (US$97 753) and Switzerland, Liechtenstein (US$93 217).

Figure 3.1.3 Distribution of world gross domestic product
(Percentage)

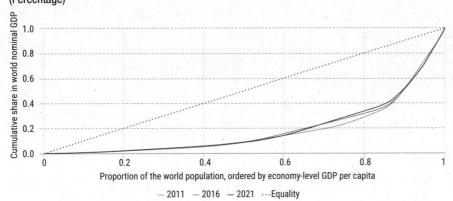

Note: Lorenz curves, as in this graph, reveal the structure of inequality. Inequality is greater the further the curve runs below the diagonal line (see annex 6.3). Inequality within economies is not considered.

World **GDP increased by 5.7%** in 2021

Growth of world **GDP nowcast** to slow down to **3.3% in 2022**

GDP growth in LDCs still below

2030 Agenda target of 7%

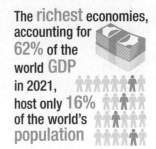

The **richest** economies, accounting for **62%** of the world GDP in 2021, host only **16%** of the world's **population**

45

Table 3.1.1 | **Gross domestic product and gross domestic product per capita**

Group of economies	Value		Annual growth rate			
	Nominal GDP	Nominal GDP per capita	Real GDP[a]		Real GDP[a] per capita	
	(Billions of US$)	(US$)	(Percentage)		(Percentage)	
	2021	2021	2020	2021	2020	2021
World	**96 241**	**12 170**	**-3.4**	**5.7**	**-4.3**	**4.7**
Developed economies	57 964	43 149	-4.4	5.0	-4.6	4.9
Developing economies	38 277	5 831	-1.8	6.7	-2.9	5.6
Developing economies: Africa	2 666	1 915	-2.7	5.0	-5.0	2.5
Developing economies: Americas	5 140	7 888	-7.4	6.2	-8.1	5.5
Developing economies: Asia and Oceania	30 471	6 740	-0.5	7.0	-1.3	6.2
Selected groups						
Developing economies excluding China	20 978	4 082	-4.8	5.6	-6.1	4.2
Developing economies excluding LDCs	37 076	6 784	-1.8	6.9	-2.7	6.0
LDCs	1 201	1 092	-0.0	2.0	-2.4	-0.4
LLDCs	900	1 635	-1.3	4.2	-3.7	1.8
SIDS (UN-OHRLLS)	814	11 732	-6.8	5.2	-7.7	4.3
HIPCs (IMF)	827	1 018	0.5	4.1	-2.3	1.3
BRICS	24 221	7 447	-0.0	7.6	-0.6	7.1
G20	82 588	16 806	-3.3	5.9	-3.8	5.5

[a] In constant 2015 United States dollars.

Table 3.1.2 | **Nominal gross domestic product by type of expenditure, 2020**
(Percentage)

Group of economies	Final consumption		Gross capital formation	Net exports of goods and services
	Households[a]	Government[b]		
World	**55.4**	**17.5**	**26.4**	**0.8**
Developed economies	58.6	18.8	22.2	0.3
Developing economies	50.2	15.5	33.1	1.5
Developing economies: Africa	69.1	13.8	22.7	-5.7
Developing economies: Americas	64.2	16.9	17.2	0.8
Developing economies: Asia and Oceania	46.0	15.4	36.8	2.2
Selected groups				
Developing economies excluding China	59.8	14.7	24.6	0.5
Developing economies excluding LDCs	49.5	15.7	33.3	1.8
LDCs	71.1	10.7	26.4	-7.9
LLDCs	63.9	13.9	26.9	-5.6
SIDS (UN-OHRLLS)	48.4	17.8	20.7	12.9
HIPCs (IMF)	71.2	11.8	25.1	-7.8
BRICS	44.2	16.2	38.1	2.3
G20	54.8	17.9	26.7	0.7

[a] Including non-profit institutions serving households.
[b] General government.

Table 3.1.3 | **Nominal gross value added by economic activity**
(Percentage)

Group of economies	Agriculture		Industry		Services	
	2010	2020	2010	2020	2010	2020
World	**4.1**	**4.5**	**29.1**	**27.3**	**66.8**	**68.2**
Developed economies	1.5	1.4	24.6	22.8	73.9	75.7
Developing economies	9.5	9.4	38.8	34.2	51.7	56.4
Developing economies: Africa	15.1	17.5	34.0	29.5	50.9	53.0
Developing economies: Americas	5.3	6.3	32.1	27.4	62.5	66.3
Developing economies: Asia and Oceania	10.2	9.2	41.8	35.7	48.0	55.1
Selected groups						
Developing economies excluding China	9.4	10.6	35.6	30.9	55.1	58.4
Developing economies excluding LDCs	9.0	9.0	39.1	34.4	51.8	56.7
LDCs	24.1	21.2	29.1	29.8	46.9	49.1
LLDCs	16.9	17.9	35.6	31.4	47.5	50.7
SIDS (UN-OHRLLS)	3.3	3.4	27.8	26.5	68.9	70.1
HIPCs (IMF)	25.3	24.8	27.0	27.6	47.7	47.6
BRICS	9.3	8.8	39.4	35.3	51.3	55.9
G20	3.4	3.7	28.1	26.8	68.6	69.5

Table 3.1.4 | **Economies with highest gross domestic product per capita**

Economy	Nominal value		Real annual growth rate[a]	Structure by type of expenditure			
				Final consumption		Gross capital formation	Net exports of goods and services
				Household[b]	Government[c]		
	(US$)		(Percentage)	(Percentage)	(Percentage)	(Percentage)	(Percentage)
	2020	2021	2021	2020	2020	2020	2020
Luxembourg	116 360	132 918	3.3	30.7	18.3	17.9	33.1
Bermuda	120 552	126 972	3.9	47.2	11.8	13.9	24.9
Cayman Islands	92 944	99 007	3.5	52.7	9.6	15.7	21.5
Ireland	86 106	97 753	10.1	25.1	12.6	40.9	22.3
Switzerland, Liechtenstein	87 483	93 645	2.7	51.0	11.9	28.4	8.8
Norway	67 385	88 792	2.8	43.8	26.5	30.1	-0.4
Qatar	53 036	69 066	6.3	26.2	23.3	42.4	8.1
Iceland	59 231	68 448	2.4	51.3	27.8	21.6	-0.7
United States of America	61 880	67 904	5.4	67.2	14.7	21.1	-3.0
Denmark	61 124	67 348	3.2	46.0	24.7	22.9	6.5

Note: Economies are ranked by the nominal value in 2021.
[a] In constant 2015 United States dollars.
[b] Including non-profit institutions serving households.
[c] General government.

3.2 Current account

Map 3.2 Current account balance as a ratio to gross domestic product, 2021
(Percentage)

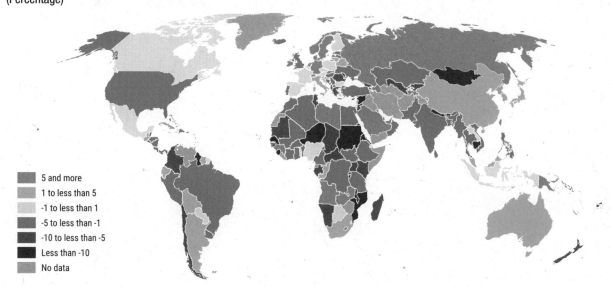

- 5 and more
- 1 to less than 5
- -1 to less than 1
- -5 to less than -1
- -10 to less than -5
- Less than -10
- No data

Concepts and definitions

The current account, within the balance of payments, displays the transactions between residents and non-residents of a reporting economy, involving economic values, namely the cross-national exchange of goods and services as well as cross-national transfers of primary and secondary income.

The current account balance shows the difference between the sum of exports and income receivable, and the sum of imports and income payable, where exports and imports refer to both goods and services, while income refers to both primary and secondary income. A surplus in the current account is recorded when receipts exceed payments; a deficit is recorded when payments exceed receipts.

The current account data in this section correspond to the latest reporting standard, known as BPM6, defined by the International Monetary Fund (IMF, 2009).

Current account imbalances across the world

Receipts earned by economies from transactions with other economies often differ significantly from the payments made. In 2021, for most economies in the Americas, Africa, South-Eastern Europe, and Central and Western Asia, payments exceeded receipts, leading to negative current account balances. Higher surpluses were found mainly in Central and Northern Europe, Eastern Asia, and Oceania. Most economies in Europe and South-Eastern Asia recorded relatively balanced current accounts.

Figure 3.2.1 Balances in the current account
(Billions of United States dollars)

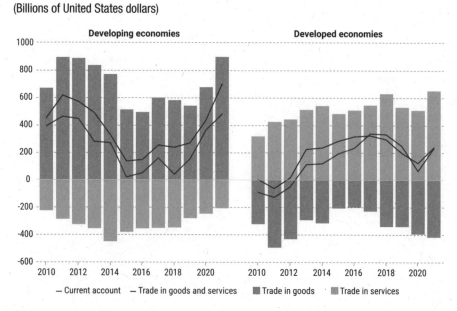

— Current account — Trade in goods and services ■ Trade in goods ■ Trade in services

Note: Current account deficits and surpluses do not add up to zero at the world level, due to imperfect geographic coverage and cross-country differences in compilation methods.

In 2021, Guinea and Papua New Guinea recorded the highest current account surpluses relative to GDP (above 20 per cent). Singapore, Kiribati, Kuwait, and Azerbaijan enjoyed surpluses of over 15 per cent of their respective GDP.

In absolute terms, the United States of America (US$822 billion) and the United Kingdom (US$83 billion) ran the world's largest current account deficits. China (US$317 billion) recorded the largest absolute surplus, followed by Germany (US$314 billion) and Japan (US$142 billion).

In 2021, the current account surplus of developing economies stood at US$480 billion, more than triple the amount recorded for 2019 (US$152 billion). Geographically, the increase in the current account balance can largely be attributed to a growing surplus in developing economies of Asia and Oceania. This group of economies recorded about US$100 billion rise each year since 2018. This was combined with a shrinking deficit in developing economies in America. The current account surplus of developed economies was recorded at US$230 billion in 2021.

Figure 3.2.2 Balances in least developed countries' current account
(Billions of United States dollars)

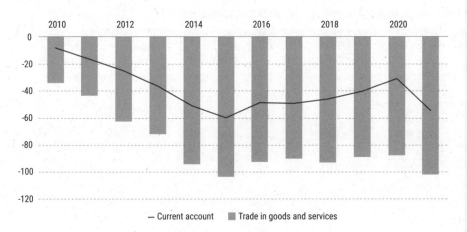

— Current account　　■ Trade in goods and services

Least developed countries' deficit up in 2021

After five years of almost continuous decline of LDCs' current account deficit since 2015, resulting in its reduction by almost a half, from US$60 billion to US$31 in 2020, in 2021, their current account deficit rose again to US$55 billion. The trade deficit also increased, surpassing US$100 billion.

Greater relative current account deficit, accounting for 4.6 per cent of GDP in 2021, distinguishes LDCs from other developing economies, which, as a group, ran a surplus of 1.3 per cent of GDP. Higher deficits relative to GDP were registered for the groups of heavily indebted poor countries (HIPCs) (3.7 per cent) and landlocked developing countries (LLDCs) (2.9 per cent). As a group, SIDS registered a comfortable 9 per cent surplus. Yet, some SIDS faced deficits close to, or over, 25 per cent of GDP.

Developing economies' surplus tripled from 2019 to 2021 – to US$480 billion

x3

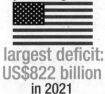

United States of America keeps having world's largest deficit: US$822 billion in 2021

Current account deficit larger than

$\frac{1}{4}$ of GDP in some SIDS

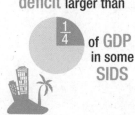

LDCs' deficit shrank from 2015 to 2020, then increased again in 2021

Table 3.2.1 | Current account balance by group of economies

Group of economies	Value (Billions of US$)			Ratio to GDP (Percentage)		
	2017–2021[a]	2020	2021	2017–2021[a]	2020	2021
World	**481**	**428**	**710**	**0.5**	**0.5**	**0.7**
Developed economies	243	64	230	0.5	0.1	0.4
Developing economies	239	364	480	0.7	1.1	1.3
Developing economies: Africa	-72	-88	-41	-2.9	-3.6	-1.6
Developing economies: Americas	-82	-1	-77	-1.5	-0.0	-1.5
Developing economies: Asia and Oceania	393	452	598	1.5	1.7	2.0
Selected groups						
Developing economies excluding China	62	115	162	0.3	0.6	0.8
Developing economies excluding LDCs	283	395	534	0.8	1.2	1.4
LDCs	-44	-31	-55	-3.9	-2.7	-4.6
LLDCs	-29	-28	-26	-3.5	-3.4	-2.9
SIDS (UN-OHRLLS)	57	49	71	7.5	6.8	9.0
HIPCs (IMF)	-34	-26	-30	-4.6	-3.4	-3.7
BRICS	184	300	392	0.8	1.5	1.6
G20	253	251	391	0.3	0.3	0.5

Note: Current account deficits and surpluses do not add up to zero at the world level, due to imperfect geographic coverage and cross-country differences in compilation methods.
[a] Annual average.

Table 3.2.2 | Current account balance in largest surplus and deficit economies

Economy (Ranked by 2021 value)	2017–2021[a]		2020		2021	
	Value (Billions of US$)	Ratio to GDP (Percentage)	Value (Billions of US$)	Ratio to GDP (Percentage)	Value (Billions of US$)	Ratio to GDP (Percentage)
China	176	1.2	249	1.7	317	1.8
Germany	298	7.6	274	7.1	314	7.4
Japan	169	3.4	147	2.9	142	2.9
Russian Federation	74	4.4	36	2.4	122	6.9
China, Taiwan Province of	86	13.0	95	14.2	115	14.6
⋮	⋮	⋮	⋮	⋮	⋮	⋮
Chile	-9	-3.0	3	1.3	-20	-6.4
Brazil	-38	-2.1	-24	-1.7	-28	-1.7
India	-27	-0.9	33	1.2	-35	-1.1
United Kingdom	-88	-3.1	-70	-2.5	-83	-2.6
United States of America	-542	-2.5	-616	-2.9	-822	-3.6

[a] Annual average.

Table 3.2.3 | Current accounts of leading exporters (goods and services) by group of economies, 2021

Developed economies

Economy (Ranked by export share)	Current account balance		Trade balance[a]	Exports[a]	Imports[a]
	Value (Billions of US$)	Ratio to GDP (Percentage)	Value (Billions of US$)	Share in world (Percentage)	Share in world (Percentage)
United States of America	-822	-3.6	-846	9.2	12.6
Germany	314	7.4	(e) 224	(e) 7.1	(e) 6.6
France	11	0.4	-36	3.3	3.6
Japan	142	2.9	(e) -24	(e) 3.3	(e) 3.5
Netherlands	97	9.6	(e) 94	(e) 3.2	(e) 3.0
Developed economies	**230**	**0.4**	**237**	**59.4**	**60.6**

[a] Goods and services.

Developing economies

Economy (Ranked by export share)	Current account balance		Trade balance[a]	Exports[a]	Imports[a]
	Value (Billions of US$)	Ratio to GDP (Percentage)	Value (Billions of US$)	Share in world (Percentage)	Share in world (Percentage)
China	317	1.8	(e) 514	(e) 12.9	(e) 11.5
China, Hong Kong SAR	42	11.3	18	2.7	2.7
Singapore	72	18.7	125	2.6	2.3
India	-35	-1.1	(e) -133	2.3	(e) 2.9
Mexico	-5	-0.4	(e) -22	(e) 1.9	(e) 2.0
Developing economies	**480**	**1.3**	**699**	**40.6**	**39.4**

[a] Goods and services.

Developing economies: Africa

Economy (Ranked by export share)	Current account balance		Trade balance[a]	Exports[a]	Imports[a]
	Value (Billions of US$)	Ratio to GDP (Percentage)	Value (Billions of US$)	Share in world (Percentage)	Share in world (Percentage)
South Africa	16	4.1	26	0.5	0.4
Egypt	(e) -18	(e) -4.5	(e) -36	(e) 0.2	(e) 0.3
Nigeria	(e) -4	(e) -0.8	(e) -14	(e) 0.2	(e) 0.2
Morocco	-3	-2.5	-13	0.2	0.2
Algeria	(e) -3	(e) -2.1	(e) -1	(e) 0.1	(e) 0.2
Developing Africa	**-41**	**-1.6**	**-88**	**2.3**	**2.7**

[a] Goods and services.

Developing economies: Americas

Economy (Ranked by export share)	Current account balance		Trade balance[a]	Exports[a]	Imports[a]
	Value (Billions of US$)	Ratio to GDP (Percentage)	Value (Billions of US$)	Share in world (Percentage)	Share in world (Percentage)
Mexico	-5	-0.4	(e) -22	(e) 1.9	(e) 2.0
Brazil	-28	-1.7	19	1.1	1.1
Chile	-20	-6.4	(e) 1	(e) 0.4	(e) 0.4
Argentina	7	1.4	15	0.3	0.3
Peru	-5	-2.4	7	0.2	0.2
Developing Americas	**-77**	**-1.5**	**-48**	**4.9**	**5.3**

[a] Goods and services.

Developing economies: Asia and Oceania

Economy (Ranked by export share)	Current account balance		Trade balance[a]	Exports[a]	Imports[a]
	Value (Billions of US$)	Ratio to GDP (Percentage)	Value (Billions of US$)	Share in world (Percentage)	Share in world (Percentage)
China	317	1.8	(e) 514	(e) 12.9	(e) 11.5
China, Hong Kong SAR	42	11.3	18	2.7	2.7
Singapore	72	18.7	125	2.6	2.3
India	-35	-1.1	(e) -133	2.3	(e) 2.9
China, Taiwan Province of	115	14.6	103	1.8	1.5
Developing Asia and Oceania	**598**	**2.0**	**834**	**33.3**	**31.4**

[a] Goods and services.

3.3 Foreign direct investment

Map 3.3 Foreign direct investment inflows as a ratio to gross fixed capital formation, 2021
(Percentage)

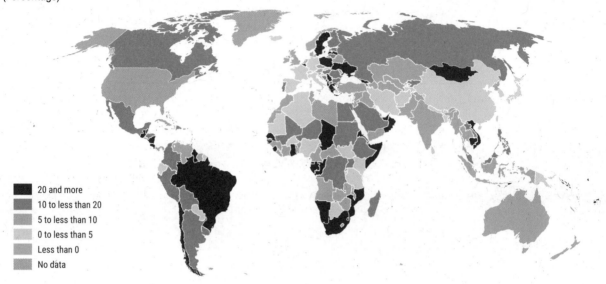

- 20 and more
- 10 to less than 20
- 5 to less than 10
- 0 to less than 5
- Less than 0
- No data

Concepts and definitions

FDI is defined as an investment reflecting a lasting interest and control by a foreign direct investor, resident in one economy, in an enterprise resident in another economy (foreign affiliate).

FDI inflows comprise capital provided by a foreign direct investor to its foreign affiliate resident in the reporting country, or capital received by a foreign direct investor resident in the reporting country from its foreign affiliate abroad.

FDI flows are presented on a net basis, i.e., as credits less debits. Thus, in cases of reverse investment or disinvestment, FDI may be negative.

FDI stock is the value of capital and reserves attributable to a non-resident parent enterprise, plus the net indebtedness of foreign affiliates to parent enterprises (UNCTAD, 2022c).

Trends and global patterns

Global FDI flows in 2021 were US$1.6 trillion, up 64.3 per cent from the exceptionally low level in 2020. The 2021 recovery brought growth in FDI in all regions. FDI as a ratio to gross fixed capital formation (GFCF) rose from 4.3 per cent in 2020 to 7.1 per cent in 2021.

Outflows by group of economies

In 2021, developed economies more than tripled their investment abroad to US$1.3 trillion, from US$408 billion in 2020. The value of FDI outflows from developing economies rose by 17.8 per cent to US$438 billion. Developing Asia and Oceania remained a major source of investment flows even during the pandemic.

Figure 3.3.1 World foreign direct investment inflows
(Billions of United States dollars)

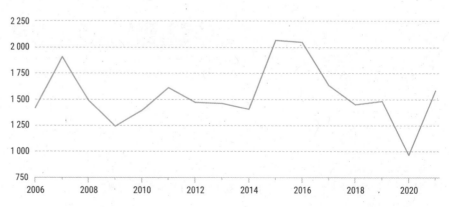

Note: Excluding financial centres in the Caribbean (see note, table 3.3.1).

Inflows by group of economies

FDI flows to developing economies grew more slowly than those to developed economies but still increased by 29.9 per cent, to US$837 billion. FDI flows to Africa reached US$83 billion – a record level – from US$39 billion in 2020, more than doubling the 2020 level. In developing Asia and Oceania, FDI inflows rose to an all-time high for the third consecutive year, reaching US$619 billion, an increase of 19.3 per cent. In developing economies in the Americas, FDI inflows rose by 56 per cent to US$134 billion, recovering part of the ground lost in 2020.

Figure 3.3.2 Foreign direct investment inflows and outflows, 2021
(Billions of United States dollars)

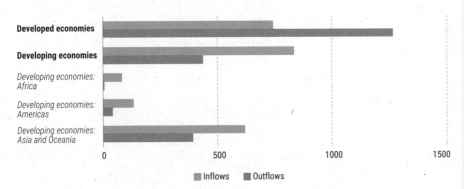

Note: Excluding financial centres in the Caribbean (see note, table 3.3.1).

Origins and destinations of foreign direct investment

In 2021, the share of global inflows accounted for by developed economies returned to pre-pandemic levels, at about half of the total, from just one third in 2020. The share of developing economies in global flows remained just above 50 per cent. FDI flows to Africa accounted for 5.2 per cent of global FDI and FDI to developing Asia and Oceania, the largest recipient region of FDI, accounted for 39.1 per cent of global inflows.

The share of developed economies in global outward FDI flows rose from 52.3 per cent in 2020 to 74.3 per cent in 2021, while the share of developing economies dropped from 47.7 per cent to 25.7 per cent. Developed Europe was the largest source of global FDI outflows (32.3 per cent), followed by the developed economies in the Americas (28.9 per cent).

Figure 3.3.3 Selected foreign direct investment flows
(Percentage of world total)

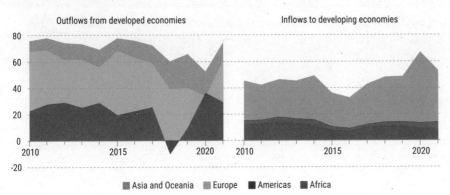

Note: Excluding financial centres in the Caribbean (see note, table 3.3.1).

Global FDI inflows rose by 64% to US$1.6 trillion in 2021

FDI inflows to developed economies more than doubled in 2021

+133%

39% of global FDI inflows to developing Asia, in 2021

In 2021, FDI outflows from developed economies more than tripled

53

Table 3.3.1 | Foreign direct investment flows by group of economies

Group of economies	Inflows				Outflows			
	Value		Annual growth rate		Value		Annual growth rate	
	(Billions of US$)		(Percentage)		(Billions of US$)		(Percentage)	
	2020	2021	2020	2021	2020	2021	2020	2021
World[a]	963	1 582	-35.0	64.3	780	1 708	-30.6	118.8
Developed economies	319	746	-58.2	133.6	408	1 269	-44.6	210.9
Developing economies	644	837	-10.1	29.9	372	438	-3.8	17.8
Developing economies: Africa	39	83	-14.7	113.1	-1	3	-112.7	-526.2
Developing economies: Americas	86	134	-45.7	56.0	-5	42	-110.0	-995.6
Developing economies: Asia and Oceania	519	619	1.4	19.3	378	394	12.6	4.3
Selected groups								
Developing economies excluding China	495	656	-14.0	32.6	219	293	-12.6	34.1
Developing economies excluding LDCs	621	811	-10.4	30.5	371	439	-4.5	18.3
LDCs	23	26	0.6	13.1	2	0	-250.1	-109.4
LLDCs	14	18	-35.9	30.7	-1	2	-271.4	-231.6
SIDS (UN-OHRLLS)	82	107	-28.9	30.5	31	48	-42.7	51.3
HIPCs (IMF)	24	32	-12.1	33.6	1	2	-44.0	65.3
BRICS	255	355	-13.3	39.2	157	247	-19.3	57.9
G20	757	1 104	-34.7	45.9	596	1 496	-38.8	150.9

Note: Excluding financial centres in the Caribbean, namely: Anguilla, Antigua and Barbuda, Aruba, the Bahamas, Barbados, British Virgin Islands, Cayman Islands, Curaçao, Dominica, Grenada, Montserrat, Saint Kitts and Nevis, Saint Lucia, Saint Vincent and the Grenadines, Sint Maarten and Turks and Caicos Islands.
[a] At world level, recorded FDI inflows may not equal recorded FDI outflows, due to imperfect geographic coverage and cross-country differences in compilation methods.

Table 3.3.2 | Foreign direct investment stock by group of economies

Group of economies	Inward stock				Outward stock			
	Value		Share in world total		Value		Share in world total	
	(Billions of US$)		(Percentage)		(Billions of US$)		(Percentage)	
	2020	2021	2020	2021	2020	2021	2020	2021
World[a]	41 728	45 449	100.0	100.0	39 546	41 798	100.0	100.0
Developed economies	29 967	33 119	71.8	72.9	31 113	33 009	78.7	79.0
Developing economies	11 760	12 330	28.2	27.1	8 433	8 790	21.3	21.0
Developing economies: Africa	958	1 026	2.3	2.3	331	301	0.8	0.7
Developing economies: Americas	2 070	2 143	5.0	4.7	708	741	1.8	1.8
Developing economies: Asia and Oceania	8 732	9 160	20.9	20.2	7 394	7 747	18.7	18.5
Selected groups								
Developing economies excluding China	9 841	10 266	23.6	22.6	5 852	6 208	14.8	14.9
Developing economies excluding LDCs	11 367	11 915	27.2	26.2	8 410	8 767	21.3	21.0
LDCs	393	414	0.9	0.9	23	22	0.1	0.1
LLDCs	421	431	1.0	0.9	51	52	0.1	0.1
SIDS (UN-OHRLLS)	2 120	2 182	5.1	4.8	1 292	1 373	3.3	3.3
HIPCs (IMF)	379	403	0.9	0.9	25	26	0.1	0.1
BRICS	3 577	3 866	8.6	8.5	3 681	3 704	9.3	8.9
G20	32 394	35 756	77.6	78.7	32 883	34 919	83.2	83.5

Note: Excluding financial centres in the Caribbean (see note, table 3.3.1).
[a] At world level, recorded inward stocks may not equal recorded outward stocks, due to imperfect geographic coverage and cross-country differences in compilation methods.

Table 3.3.3 | **Foreign direct investment inflows, top 20 host economies, 2021**

Economy (Ranked by inflow value)	Inflows			Inward stock	
	Value	Ratio to GDP	Ratio to GFCF	Ratio to GDP	Ratio to GFCF
	(Billions of US$)	(Percentage)	(Percentage)	(Percentage)	(Percentage)
United States of America	367	1.6	8.2	58.9	303.3
China	181	1.0	2.9	11.9	32.7
China, Hong Kong SAR	141	38.0	226.9	546.1	3261.2
Singapore	99	25.7	135.7	521.1	2749.1
Canada	60	3.0	15.8	72.3	380.7
Brazil	50	3.1	21.2	36.9	249.7
India	45	1.4	6.2	16.2	71.2
South Africa	41	10.9	85.9	46.0	363.5
Russian Federation	38	2.2	11.8	29.5	161.7
Mexico	32	2.5	15.6	45.3	286.4
Germany	31	0.7	3.7	26.9	134.7
Israel	30	6.3	35.5	50.3	282.6
United Kingdom	28	0.9	5.8	82.4	555.6
Sweden	27	4.3	20.1	62.2	288.0
Belgium	26	4.3	20.5	102.4	483.7
Australia	25	1.5	7.9	44.9	243.0
Poland	25	3.7	25.0	40.3	271.0
Japan	25	0.5	1.9	5.2	20.1
United Arab Emirates	21	4.9	29.3	41.0	243.0
Indonesia	20	1.7	6.0	21.9	77.2

Note: Excluding financial centres in the Caribbean (see note, table 3.3.1).

Table 3.3.4 | **Foreign direct investment outflows, top 20 home economies, 2021**

Economy (Ranked by outflow value)	Outflows			Outward stock	
	Value	Ratio to GDP	Ratio to GFCF	Ratio to GDP	Ratio to GFCF
	(Billions of US$)	(Percentage)	(Percentage)	(Percentage)	(Percentage)
United States of America	403	1.7	9.0	42.5	218.5
Germany	152	3.6	17.9	50.6	253.3
Japan	147	3.0	11.5	40.1	155.1
China	145	0.8	2.3	14.9	40.9
United Kingdom	108	3.4	22.7	67.8	457.0
Canada	90	4.5	23.8	114.9	605.0
China, Hong Kong SAR	87	23.6	141.0	562.3	3358.2
Russian Federation	64	3.6	19.7	22.6	123.7
Ireland	62	12.7	36.7	261.3	754.8
Korea, Republic of	61	3.4	11.9	30.7	108.2
Singapore	47	12.3	64.9	349.5	1844.0
Belgium	46	7.7	36.5	117.1	553.0
Netherlands	29	2.9	14.8	333.5	1724.6
Luxembourg	25	29.9	205.3	1497.8	10290.4
Saudi Arabia	24	2.9	15.0	18.2	95.2
Brazil	23	1.4	9.7	18.5	124.8
United Arab Emirates	23	5.4	31.9	51.4	304.5
Denmark	22	5.7	28.0	68.7	338.3
Sweden	20	3.3	15.2	72.0	333.4
Thailand	17	3.4	15.0	35.1	153.0

Note: Excluding financial centres in the Caribbean (see note, table 3.3.1).

3.4 Prices

Map 3.4 Annual growth of consumer prices, 2021
(Percentage)

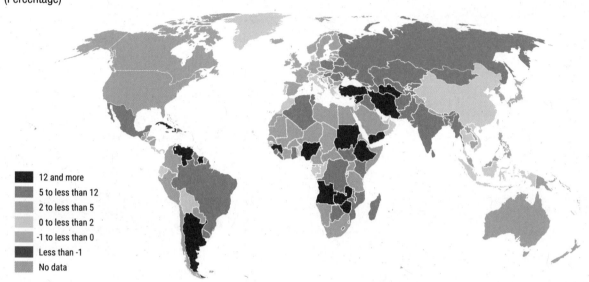

- 12 and more
- 5 to less than 12
- 2 to less than 5
- 0 to less than 2
- -1 to less than 0
- Less than -1
- No data

Concepts and definitions

Changes in consumer prices are measured by the consumer price index (CPI), which depicts the price of a basket of consumer goods and services representing average consumption by private households during a year, relative to the base year 2010.

The UNCTAD Commodity Price Index (UCPI) measures the average price, in United States dollars, of main primary commodities exported by developing economies relative to the base year 2015. The weights used in the calculation of the average price represent the shares of commodity groups in developing economies' total commodity exports observed over three years from 2014 to 2016. The overall index is decomposed into sub-indices displaying the price movements of individual commodity groups. The basket of the UCPI was entirely overhauled in 2018. For details, see annex 6.3 and UNCTAD (2018).

Growth of consumer prices worldwide

Inflation rates were above the five-year average in developing as well as developed economies in 2021. Inflation was especially high in Venezuela (+1590 per cent), Sudan (+360 per cent) and Cuba (+260 per cent). Another seven economies recorded consumer price increases of over 40 per cent and another eight over 12 per cent. The median inflation rate was 3.8 per cent among developing and 2.8 per cent among developed economies. Only seven economies experienced deflation in 2021, and only one (Samoa, -3.0 per cent) recorded a consumer price decrease of more than 1 per cent.

Trends in exchange rates

From 2020 to 2021, the yuan and the pound sterling appreciated by around 7 per cent against the United States dollar. Over the same period, appreciation of the euro was about half of that while the yen depreciated by nearly 3 per cent against the dollar.

Figure 3.4.1 Exchange rates against the United States dollar
(Annual average)

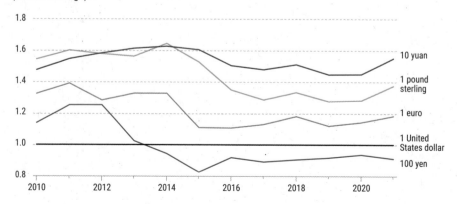

Commodity price index rose sharply, led by fuel prices

The UCPI increased by 55 per cent on an annual basis in 2021, more than any other year over the last two decades. An increase in fuel prices, increasing by 86 per cent, accounted for most of this sharp increase in the overall index. However, even excluding fuels the index rose by 23 per cent and approached its previous 2011 peak. The commodity group with the highest prices compared to the base year of 2015 was minerals, ores and non-precious metals. These have doubled in price over the last six years.

Figure 3.4.2 UNCTAD Commodity Price Index
(2015=100)

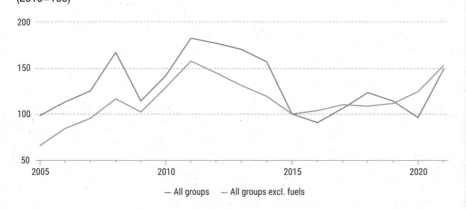

— All groups   — All groups excl. fuels

Commodity price increase continued into 2022

Since March 2021 and through the first half of 2022, fuels were over 80 per cent more expensive than twelve months earlier. Other commodity groups also recorded positive year-on-year growth in prices through most of the same period. The net effect was the UCPI in August 2022 reaching its highest levels since the UCPI was first compiled and published in 1995.

Notably, food commodity prices have consistently had a positive year-on-year growth rate throughout 2021 and into 2022. These price increases abated in the second quarter of 2022 but in August 2022 food commodities were 42 per cent dearer than in the same month two years earlier. In comparison to other commodity groups, prices of agricultural raw materials have remained relatively stable.

Figure 3.4.3 Year-on-year growth of prices by commodity group
(Percentage)

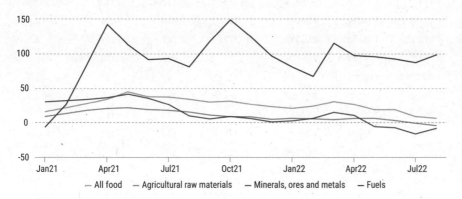

— All food   — Agricultural raw materials   — Minerals, ores and metals   — Fuels

Note: Percentage change of UCPI sub-indices, compared to the same month in the previous year.

Higher inflation all over the world in 2021 compared to the 2016 – 2020 average

¥ $ **Yuan** £ $ **and pound sterling** appreciated by 7% against the United States dollar in 2021

Fuel prices were **83% higher** in 2021 than in 2020

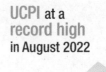

UCPI at a record high in August 2022

Table 3.4.1 | Consumer prices by group of economies

Group of economies	Consumer price index (2010=100)		Annual growth rate[a] (Percentage)	
	2016	2021	2016–2021	2021
World	**119**	**140**	**1.0**	**4.8**
Developed economies	111	122	1.0	3.4
Developing economies	135	175	1.1	6.9
Developing economies: Africa	165	334	1.1	22.7
Developing economies: Americas	150	232	1.1	15.0
Developing economies: Asia and Oceania	128	152	1.0	3.7
Selected groups				
Developing economies excluding China	146	215	1.1	11.7
Developing economies excluding LDCs	133	169	1.0	5.7
LDCs	180	440	1.2	39.3
LLDCs	155	271	1.1	11.4
SIDS (UN-OHRLLS)	120	175	1.1	32.9
HIPCs (IMF)	146	203	1.1	8.3
BRICS	129	148	1.0	2.5
G20	116	132	1.0	3.7

[a] Least squares growth rate (see annex 6.3)
Note: Venezuela is not considered.

Table 3.4.2 | Exchange rate and consumer prices among main exporting economies

Economy (Ranked by share in world exports)	Exchange rate to United States dollar			Consumer price index (2010=100)			Share in world exports[a] (Percentage)
	2019	2020	2021	2019	2020	2021	2021
China	0.14475	0.14491	0.15506	125	128	129	(e) 12.9
United States of America	1.00000	1.00000	1.00000	117	119	124	9.2
Germany	1.11947	1.14220	1.18274	114	114	118	(e) 7.1
France	1.11947	1.14220	1.18274	(e) 112	(e) 112	(e) 114	3.3
Japan	0.00917	0.00937	0.00911	105	105	105	(e) 3.3
Netherlands	1.11947	1.14220	1.18274	115	116	119	(e) 3.2
United Kingdom	1.27641	1.28205	1.37539	121	122	125	3.1
Korea, Republic of	0.00086	0.00085	0.00087	115	116	119	(e) 2.8
China, Hong Kong SAR	0.12762	0.12891	0.12865	135	135	137	2.7
Singapore	0.73305	0.72477	0.74433	114	114	117	2.6
Italy	1.11947	1.14220	1.18274	111	111	113	2.5
Ireland	1.11947	1.14220	1.18274	106	105	108	2.4
India	0.01420	0.01350	0.01353	172	182	192	2.3
Canada	0.75370	0.74563	0.79753	117	118	122	(e) 2.2
Switzerland, Liechtenstein	1.00633	1.06500	1.09428	100	99	99	2.0
Russian Federation	0.01545	0.01387	0.01358	181	187	199	(e) 2.0
Mexico	0.05191	0.04654	0.04933	142	146	155	(e) 1.9
Belgium	1.11947	1.14220	1.18274	117	118	121	1.8
China, Taiwan Province of	0.03233	0.03380	0.03568	109	109	111	1.8
Spain	1.11947	1.14220	1.18274	111	111	114	1.8

[a] Exports of goods and services.

Table 3.4.3 | **Price indices of selected primary commodities**
(2015=100)

Commodity group	2011	2012	2013	2014	2015	2016	2017	2018	2019	2020	2021
All groups	**182**	**177**	**170**	**157**	**100**	**91**	**106**	**123**	**114**	**96**	**149**
All food	141	132	120	119	100	104	102	96	94	100	130
Food	135	127	120	118	100	104	103	96	98	102	121
Tropical beverages	144	112	90	111	100	97	94	86	81	85	109
Vegetable oilseeds and oils	151	152	136	123	100	107	106	100	93	106	157
Agricultural raw materials	177	143	131	115	100	100	105	103	99	97	110
Minerals, ores and metals	164	153	138	121	100	105	116	118	125	145	175
Minerals, ores and non-precious metals	191	159	156	133	100	101	128	131	135	140	201
Precious metals	143	148	125	111	100	107	108	108	117	148	153
Fuels	198	197	194	180	100	83	104	133	116	79	146
Selected groups											
Tropical beverages and food	137	124	112	117	100	102	101	94	94	98	118
All groups excl. fuels	158	145	131	119	100	104	110	109	112	124	153
All groups excl. precious metals	188	181	176	163	100	88	106	126	114	89	148
All groups excl. precious metals and fuels	164	143	134	123	100	102	112	109	109	114	153

Table 3.4.4 | **Monthly price indices of main commodity groups**
(2015=100)

	Period	All groups	All food	Agricultural raw materials	Minerals, ores and metals	Fuels
2021	January	**121**	118	108	171	105
	February	**132**	121	110	171	122
	March	**130**	122	111	169	119
	April	**131**	126	109	175	119
	May	**141**	134	110	189	128
	June	**147**	131	110	188	139
	July	**152**	131	109	186	147
	August	**149**	133	110	174	146
	September	**160**	132	109	166	166
	October	**177**	136	111	170	193
	November	**173**	137	113	166	186
	December	**173**	137	112	168	186
2022	January	**177**	143	114	175	189
	February	**189**	150	116	181	204
	March	**225**	159	116	194	256
	April	**211**	159	116	193	234
	May	**217**	159	117	177	249
	June	**226**	155	113	174	266
	July	**225**	142	108	156	274
	August	**235**	141	105	160	289

4

POPULATION

KEY FIGURES **2021**

World population
7.9 billion

Annual
population growth
+0.9%

Share of urban
population in
developing economies
52%

Child dependency
ratio in LDCs
68%

4.1 Total and urban population

Map 4.1 Annual population growth, 2021
(Percentage)

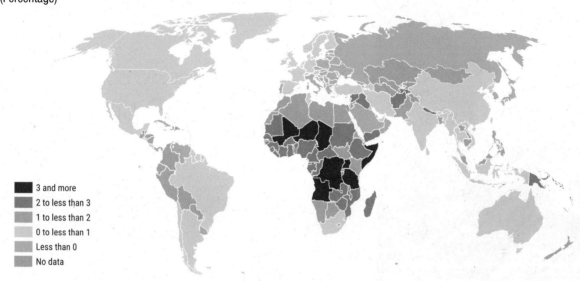

- 3 and more
- 2 to less than 3
- 1 to less than 2
- 0 to less than 1
- Less than 0
- No data

Concepts and definitions

The population estimates and projections reported in this chapter were made in 2022 and represent the population present in an economy (including residents, migrants and refugees) as of 1 July of a given year (UN DESA, 2022a, 2022b).

The figures for the years from 2022 to 2050 are based on the medium fertility variant projection. The assumptions for these projections imply that the average fertility rate of the world will decline from 2.3 births per woman in 2021 to 2.1 in 2050. The United Nations also produce other projection variants. Their outcome is highly dependent on the path that future fertility takes (UN DESA, 2022b).

Urban population is defined as the population living in areas classified as urban according to the criteria used by each country or territory. The latest estimates and projections for urban population were made in 2018 (UN DESA, 2018, 2019).

Slowdown of world population growth

The world population is estimated to have grown by 0.9 per cent in 2021 and is projected to surpass 8 billion in 2022. The growth rate has slowed down faster since the outbreak of the COVID-19 pandemic in 2020 than during the gradual slowdown taking place from the late 1980s. It is expected to rebound in 2023 before continuing its decent towards a forecast 0.5 per cent growth in 2050.

A population decrease was seen in 52 economies in 2021. The population of 22 of those was growing five years earlier. Of these economies with newly negative population growth, 11 were expected to still have decreasing populations in 2026. The last group includes Montserrat, San Marino, Belarus, Cuba, North Macedonia and Russian Federation.

The population of Africa is growing much faster than that of any other continent. Of the 30 economies with the fastest growing population, only Afghanistan, the Syrian Arab Republic and Solomon Islands are outside Africa.

Figure 4.1.1 Annual growth rate of world population
(Percentage)

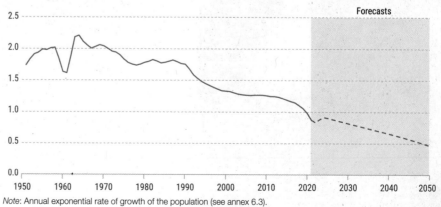

Note: Annual exponential rate of growth of the population (see annex 6.3).

Developing economies drive population growth

Over the last 25 years, the world population has increased by 2.1 billion people. Almost all this growth has occurred in developing economies, mainly in Asia and Oceania (+1.2 billion) and Africa (+0.7 billion). In 2021, five in six people in the world lived in a developing economy.

In the coming 25 years, global population is projected to grow by 1.6 billion people. The population of the economies that are today considered developing will continue to grow. Africa is expected to lead this growth (+0.9 billion) followed by developing economies in Asia and Oceania (+0.6 billion).

Figure 4.1.2 World population by group of economies
(Billions)

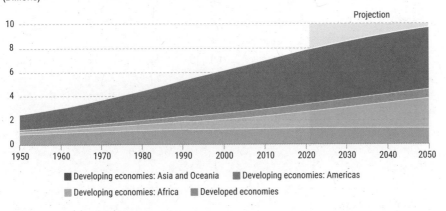

Developing economies: Asia and Oceania   Developing economies: Americas
Developing economies: Africa   Developed economies

Urbanization continues

All over the world, a growing proportion of the population lives in cities. In 2011, 52.0 per cent lived in urban areas. The share of urban population was projected to have increased to 56.5 per cent in 2021. It is generally higher in the developed (79.5 per cent in 2021) than in the developing world (51.8 per cent). In LDCs, the people living in urban areas are in the minority (35.3 per cent).

Over the last ten years, urbanization has been most pronounced in developing economies, especially in Asia and Oceania, which saw the urban rate increase from 43.3 in 2011 to 50.0 per cent in 2021. Africa has seen a 4.6 percentage point increase in the same period. By contrast, further urbanization in the developing economies of the Americas has been relatively modest. Urbanization levels in this region are already comparable to developed economies.

Figure 4.1.3 Urban population by group of economies
(Percentage of total population)

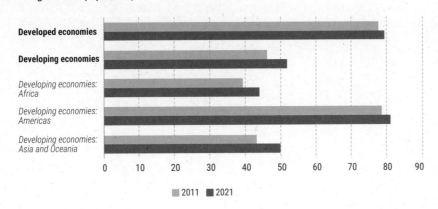

2011   2021

World **population** projected to surpass 8 billion in 2022

World population growth rate dipped down to

0.9%

in 2021

Five in six people

live in a developing economy

57% of the world's population live in urban areas

Table 4.1.1 | Total population by group of economies

Group of economies	Population (Millions)			Annual growth rate[a] (Percentage)		
	2016	2021	2050	2016–2021	2021	2021–2050
World	**7 513**	**7 909**	**9 709**	**1.0**	**0.9**	**0.7**
Developed economies	1 329	1 343	1 332	0.2	0.0	-0.0
Developing economies	6 184	6 566	8 377	1.2	1.0	0.8
Developing economies: Africa	1 231	1 392	2 483	2.5	2.4	2.0
Developing economies: Americas	625	652	745	0.8	0.7	0.5
Developing economies: Asia and Oceania	4 329	4 521	5 149	0.9	0.7	0.4
Selected groups						
Developing economies excluding China	4 783	5 140	7 065	1.4	1.3	1.1
Developing economies excluding LDCs	5 209	5 466	6 449	1.0	0.8	0.6
LDCs	975	1 100	1 928	2.4	2.4	1.9
LLDCs	490	551	954	2.4	2.4	1.9
SIDS (UN-OHRLLS)	66	70	84	1.0	0.9	0.6
HIPCs (IMF)	706	812	1 559	2.8	2.7	2.3
BRICS	3 149	3 252	3 421	0.6	0.4	0.2
G20	4 771	4 914	5 181	0.6	0.4	0.2

[a] Annual exponential rate of growth (see annex 6.3).

Table 4.1.2 | Urban population by group of economies

Group of economies	Urban population (Millions)			Share in total population (Percentage)		
	2016	2021	2050	2016	2021	2050
World	**4 081**	**4 470**	**6 605**	**54.3**	**56.5**	**68.0**
Developed economies	1 044	1 068	1 153	78.6	79.5	86.6
Developing economies	3 037	3 401	5 451	49.1	51.8	65.1
Developing economies: Africa	513	613	1 463	41.7	44.0	58.9
Developing economies: Americas	500	530	654	80.1	81.3	87.7
Developing economies: Asia and Oceania	2 023	2 259	3 334	46.7	50.0	64.8
Selected groups						
Developing economies excluding China	2 241	2 510	4 400	46.9	48.8	62.3
Developing economies excluding LDCs	2 719	3 013	4 438	52.2	55.1	68.8
LDCs	318	388	1 013	32.6	35.3	52.5
LLDCs	148	174	435	30.2	31.6	45.6
SIDS (UN-OHRLLS)	39	42	56	59.4	60.5	67.4
HIPCs (IMF)	248	305	839	35.2	37.6	53.8
BRICS	1 562	1 726	2 316	49.6	53.1	67.7
G20	2 792	3 008	3 814	58.5	61.2	73.6

Table 4.1.3 | Most populated economies

Economy	Total			Urban		
	Population	Annual growth rate[a]		Share in total population	Annual growth rate[a]	
	(Millions)	(Percentage)		(Percentage)	(Percentage)	
	2021	2016–2021	2021–2050	2021	2016–2021	2021–2050
China	1 426	0.3	-0.3	62.5	2.3	0.6
India	1 408	1.0	0.6	35.4	2.3	2.0
United States of America	340	0.6	0.4	83.0	0.8	0.6
Indonesia	274	0.9	0.5	57.3	2.1	1.3
Pakistan	231	1.6	1.6	37.4	2.3	2.7
Brazil	214	0.7	0.3	87.3	1.0	0.5
Nigeria	213	2.5	2.0	52.7	4.1	2.9
Bangladesh	169	1.2	0.6	38.9	3.3	2.0
Russian Federation	145	-0.0	-0.3	74.9	0.2	0.1
Mexico	127	0.8	0.4	81.0	1.2	0.7
Japan	125	-0.4	-0.6	91.9	-0.3	-0.5
Ethiopia	120	2.7	2.0	22.2	4.9	4.0
Philippines	114	1.6	1.1	47.7	2.2	2.0
Egypt	109	1.8	1.3	42.9	1.9	2.2
Viet Nam	97	0.9	0.3	38.1	2.9	1.7
Congo, Dem. Rep. of the	96	3.3	2.8	46.2	4.6	3.9
Türkiye	88	1.1	0.4	76.3	1.7	0.8
Iran (Islamic Republic of)	85	0.9	0.4	76.6	1.6	0.8
Germany	83	0.3	-0.2	77.5	0.3	0.1
Thailand	72	0.3	-0.2	52.2	1.8	0.8

[a] Annual exponential rate of growth (see annex 6.3).

4.2 Age structure

Map 4.2 Dependency ratio, 2021
(Percentage)

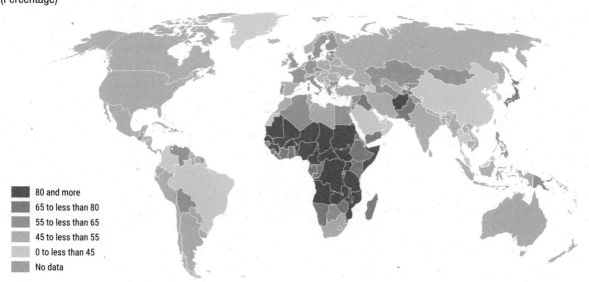

- 80 and more
- 65 to less than 80
- 55 to less than 65
- 45 to less than 55
- 0 to less than 45
- No data

Concepts and definitions

In this section, the term "persons of working age" refers to persons aged from 15 to 64 years. The term "children" refers to persons under the age of 15. The term "older persons" refers to persons over the age of 64.

The dependency ratio is defined as the number of children and older persons per hundred persons of working age. It can be expressed as the sum of the child dependency ratio and the old-age dependency ratio.

The child dependency ratio is defined as the number of children per hundred persons of working age. The old-age dependency ratio is defined as the number of older persons per hundred persons of working age.

Regional distribution of dependency ratios and trends over time

In 2021, for every 100 persons of working age there were 54 children or older people. The dependency ratio was highest in some African countries and in Afghanistan. In all these cases, the high ratios were a result of a very high child dependency. In Africa as a whole, the child dependency ratio alone was 72 per cent. By contrast, the lowest dependency ratios were found on the Arabian Peninsula and in the Caribbean. Several developed economies, most notably Japan, show rising dependency ratios due to increasing old-age dependency.

Globally, 65 per cent of people were of working age in 2021. Fifty years ago, this number was 57 per cent. The marked change is that the proportion of children has decreased from 38 per cent in 1971 to 25 per cent while the proportion of older persons has increased from 5 to 10 per cent. People above the age of 64 are projected to make up 16 per cent of the global population by 2050.

Figure 4.2.1 World population by age group
(Percentage)

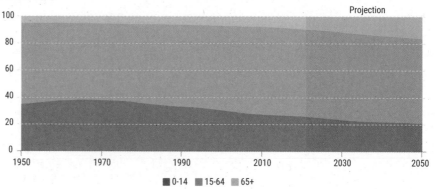

Young age cohorts are smaller in developed economies

The age structure in developing economies is pyramid shaped with older age classes successively smaller than younger classes. In developed economies, however, the biggest age groups are 30 to 59 years old. A temporarily accelerated decrease in births worldwide during the COVID-19 pandemic is reflected by the size of groups of children under 5.

Globally, in 2021, 59 per cent of people over 75 years were women, while only 48 per cent of children were girls. This imbalance in the sex distribution can be seen in both developed and developing economies.

Figure 4.2.2 **Population pyramids, 2021**
(Percentage)

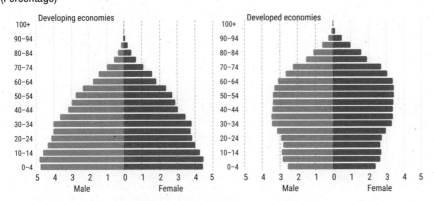

72 children
per 100 persons of
working age
in Africa

The proportion
of older persons
worldwide projected
to increase
to 16%
by 2050
from 10%
in 2021

Working age people support fewer children but more older persons

In most economies, the age structure has seen a trajectory over time, where dependency ratios first decrease, due to shrinking proportions of children, and later increase, as more people reach an age of over 64.

In most regions of the world, the bulk of the dependency ratio decrease has already taken place, and further decreases in the child dependency ratio are projected to be more than offset by increases in the old-age dependency ratio. In Africa, however, the decline of the dependency ratio is expected to continue beyond 2050. By 2050, the dependency ratio in Africa is projected to fall to 60 per cent from 78 per cent in 2021. In developed economies, dependency ratios are already increasing and are projected to reach 73 per cent by 2050.

48% of the world's
children are girls

Figure 4.2.3 **Dependency ratio by age structure**
(Percentage)

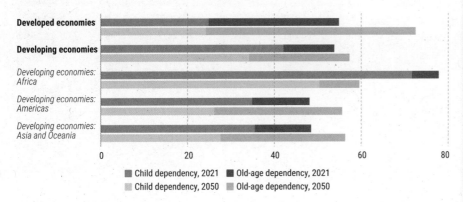

■ Child dependency, 2021   ■ Old-age dependency, 2021
□ Child dependency, 2050   □ Old-age dependency, 2050

Note: The total dependency ratio is the sum of the child and old-age dependency ratios.

Developed economies
projected to
overtake Africa
in dependency ratio
by 2050

Table 4.2.1 | Age structure and dependency ratio by group of economies

Group of economies	Year	Population (Millions)			Dependency ratio (Percentage)		
		0—14	15—64	65+	Child (0-14)	Old-age (65+)	Total
World	**1950**	**868**	**1 503**	**128**	**57.7**	**8.5**	**66.2**
	2021	**2 015**	**5 133**	**761**	**39.3**	**14.8**	**54.1**
	2050	**2 010**	**6 096**	**1 603**	**33.0**	**26.3**	**59.3**
Developed economies	1950	241	552	64	43.6	11.7	55.2
	2021	216	867	261	24.9	30.1	55.0
	2050	187	771	374	24.3	48.4	72.7
Developing economies	1950	627	952	64	65.9	6.7	72.6
	2021	1 799	4 266	500	42.2	11.7	53.9
	2050	1 823	5 325	1 229	34.2	23.1	57.3
Developing economies: Africa	1950	94	125	8	75.3	6.0	81.3
	2021	562	782	48	71.8	6.2	78.0
	2050	786	1 555	142	50.5	9.1	59.7
Developing economies: Americas	1950	68	92	5	73.8	5.8	79.6
	2021	154	440	58	35.0	13.2	48.2
	2050	126	479	141	26.3	29.4	55.7
Developing economies: Asia and Oceania	1950	465	734	51	63.3	7.0	70.3
	2021	1 083	3 044	394	35.6	13.0	48.5
	2050	911	3 291	947	27.7	28.8	56.5
Selected groups							
Developing economies excluding China	1950	438	624	36	70.1	5.8	76.0
	2021	1 547	3 279	313	47.2	9.5	56.7
	2050	1 673	4 557	834	36.7	18.3	55.0
Developing economies excluding LDCs	1950	546	843	57	64.7	6.8	71.6
	2021	1 371	3 635	461	37.7	12.7	50.4
	2050	1 228	4 110	1 111	29.9	27.0	56.9
LDCs	1950	81	109	7	74.8	6.0	80.8
	2021	429	631	40	67.9	6.3	74.2
	2050	595	1 215	119	48.9	9.8	58.7
LLDCs	1950	32	42	2	76.8	5.6	82.4
	2021	217	314	20	68.9	6.3	75.2
	2050	290	607	56	47.8	9.2	57.0
SIDS (UN-OHRLLS)	1950	8	12	1	70.2	6.4	76.6
	2021	18	46	6	39.1	12.1	51.3
	2050	17	54	13	31.7	24.1	55.7
HIPCs (IMF)	1950	53	69	4	76.7	6.1	82.7
	2021	345	443	23	78.0	5.3	83.2
	2050	517	970	72	53.3	7.4	60.7
BRICS	1950	406	692	51	58.6	7.4	66.0
	2021	700	2 222	330	31.5	14.8	46.4
	2050	523	2 161	736	24.2	34.1	58.3
G20	1950	641	1 187	106	54.0	8.9	63.0
	2021	1 014	3 307	593	30.7	17.9	48.6
	2050	794	3 220	1 167	24.7	36.2	60.9

Table 4.2.2 | Age structure by group of economies, 2021

Group of economies	Population (Millions)	Percentage of total						
		All age classes	0–14	15–24	25–39	40–64	65–74	75+
World	**7 909**	**100.0**	**25.5**	**15.5**	**22.2**	**27.2**	**6.0**	**3.6**
Developed economies	1 343	100.0	16.1	11.2	19.7	33.6	10.7	8.7
Developing economies	6 566	100.0	27.4	16.4	22.8	25.9	5.1	2.5
Developing economies: Africa	1 392	100.0	40.4	19.2	20.5	16.5	2.4	1.0
Developing economies: Americas	652	100.0	23.6	16.4	23.5	27.7	5.6	3.3
Developing economies: Asia and Oceania	4 521	100.0	24.0	15.5	23.3	28.5	5.8	2.9
Selected groups								
Developing economies excluding China	5 140	100.0	30.1	17.8	22.8	23.2	4.1	2.0
LDCs	1 100	100.0	39.0	19.9	20.8	16.7	2.5	1.1
LLDCs	551	100.0	39.3	19.6	20.9	16.6	2.5	1.0
SIDS (UN-OHRLLS)	70	100.0	25.9	16.4	22.9	26.8	5.2	2.9
Selected economies								
China	1 426	100.0	17.7	11.3	22.6	35.3	8.7	4.4
India	1 408	100.0	25.7	18.1	24.1	25.3	4.6	2.2
Brazil	214	100.0	20.5	15.4	24.2	30.3	6.2	3.3
Nigeria	213	100.0	43.3	19.6	18.9	15.2	2.1	0.8
Russian Federation	145	100.0	17.7	9.8	22.7	34.1	9.9	5.7
Japan	125	100.0	11.8	9.3	15.7	33.4	13.9	15.8

Table 4.2.3 | Female population by age class, 2021

Group of economies	Population (Millions)	Percentage female						
		All age classes	0–14	15–24	25–39	40–64	65–74	75+
World	**3 933**	**49.7**	**48.5**	**48.4**	**48.9**	**50.2**	**53.5**	**59.4**
Developed economies	689	51.2	48.7	48.7	49.3	50.9	54.4	60.8
Developing economies	3 244	49.4	48.4	48.4	48.8	50.0	53.2	58.3
Developing economies: Africa	697	50.1	49.4	49.6	50.0	51.1	54.6	58.9
Developing economies: Americas	331	50.7	49.0	49.3	50.1	51.7	54.5	59.4
Developing economies: Asia and Oceania	2 216	49.0	47.8	47.8	48.3	49.6	52.8	58.1
Selected groups								
Developing economies excluding China	2 546	49.5	48.7	48.8	49.1	50.1	53.3	58.5
LDCs	553	50.3	49.3	49.6	50.6	51.7	54.4	57.3
LLDCs	277	50.3	49.2	49.6	50.6	52.0	56.2	61.1
SIDS (UN-OHRLLS)	34	49.4	48.9	48.8	48.6	49.6	52.3	57.5
Selected economies								
China	698	48.9	46.4	46.2	47.7	49.7	53.0	58.1
India	681	48.4	47.8	47.5	48.0	48.9	51.0	55.6
Brazil	109	50.9	49.0	49.2	49.9	51.8	55.5	60.3
Nigeria	106	49.5	49.3	49.1	49.4	50.0	51.8	53.0
Russian Federation	78	53.6	48.7	49.0	49.7	53.9	62.9	73.7
Japan	64	51.4	48.9	48.9	49.0	49.7	52.0	60.2

MARITIME
TRANSPORT

KEY FIGURES **2021**

Seaborne trade
volume

11 billion tons

Change of
seaborne trade

+3.2%

World commercial
fleet capacity
(as of 31 December)

2.2 billion dwt

Registered
port calls

4.3 million

5.1 World seaborne trade

Map 5.1 Tonnage loaded and discharged, 2021
(Billions of metric tons)

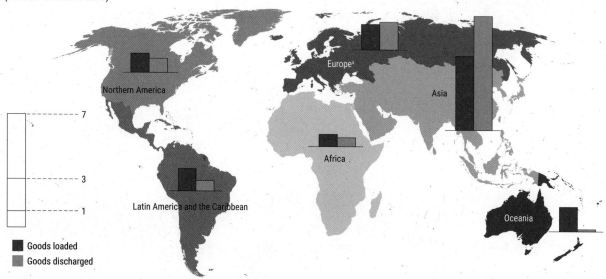

- Goods loaded
- Goods discharged

[a] Including the Russian Federation and the French overseas departments.

Concepts and definitions

The figures on seaborne trade in this section measure the volumes of international shipments, in metric tons, of goods loaded and discharged in the world's seaports. Cabotage and transshipments are not included.

Goods loaded for international shipment are assumed to be exports, while goods discharged from ships are assumed to be imports. The seaborne trade balance measures the difference between the volumes of loaded and discharged goods.

Dry cargo refers to cargo that is usually not carried in tankers, such as dry bulks (e.g., coal, ores, grains), pallets, bags, crates, and containers. "Other" tanker trade refers to tanker trade, excluding crude oil. It includes refined petroleum products, gas and chemicals.

The data presented in this section have been compiled from various sources, including country reports as well as port industry and other specialist websites (see UNCTAD 2022d).

Trends and geography of world seaborne trade in 2021

Having contracted by nearly four per cent in 2020 on the back of the COVID-19 pandemic, international maritime trade recovered in 2021 as volumes bounced back at an estimated rate of 3.2 per cent. Shipments reached 11.0 billion tons, a value slightly below pre-pandemic levels.

In 2021, Asia remained the world-leading maritime freight area with Asian ports, including in developed and developing regions, loading around 4.6 billion tons of goods, or about 42 per cent of total goods loaded in ports worldwide. About 7.1 billion tons, equivalent to 64 per cent of total goods discharged worldwide, were received by Asian ports in 2021.

A key trend in maritime trade is the shift in cargo composition. In 1970, more than half of global seaborne trade was tanker cargo. Today, almost three-quarters of loaded goods are dry cargo, including bulk and cargo shipped in containers. Of the total maritime freight shipped internationally in 2021, 8.0 billion tons was dry cargo.

Figure 5.1.1 Goods loaded worldwide
(Billions of tons)

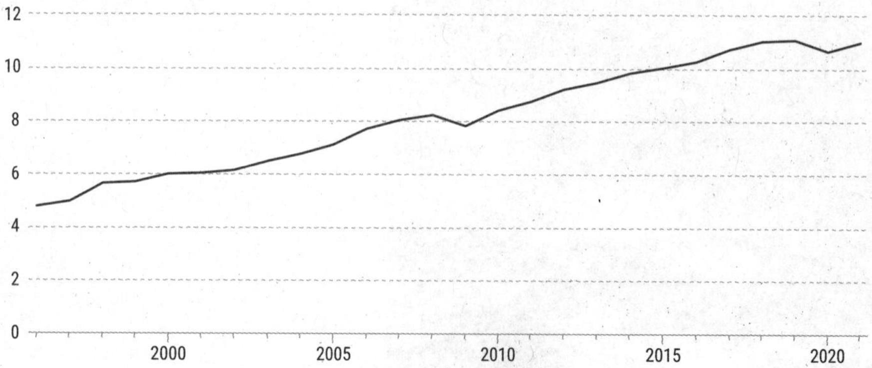

Contribution of developing economies

In 2021, developing economies still accounted for the largest share of global seaborne trade. They loaded 55 per cent and discharged 61 per cent of the world total. Asian developing economies held the lion's share. Participation in globalized manufacturing and containerized trade has generally been concentrated in Asia, notably in China and neighbouring East Asian economies. Other developing regions did not contribute equally, a reflection of their varying degrees of integration into global value chains and manufacturing networks.

Figure 5.1.2 Seaborne trade of developing economies
(Percentage of corresponding world tonnage)

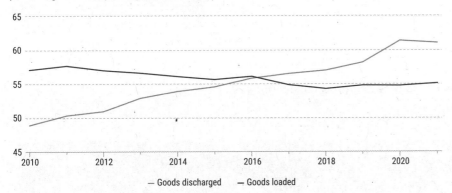

— Goods discharged   — Goods loaded

Developments in seaborne trade balances

Developing economies still reported a maritime trade deficit in 2021 while developed economies featured a surplus. In 2016, developing economies discharged 4 million tons more goods than they loaded. This deficit deepened to 648 million tons in 2021. On the other hand, the surplus in developed economies reached 658 million tons in 2021. This is a reversal of roles from 2010 when developing economies had a maritime trade surplus of 706 million tons while developed economies discharged 669 million tons more than they loaded.

The maritime trade deficit for developing economies can be attributed to discharging dry cargo including bulk and containerized goods more than loading. This in turn is concentrated to the developing economies of Asia. For other cargo types and in other geographical areas developing economies often have a maritime trade surplus.

Figure 5.1.3 Seaborne trade balance
(Millions of tons)

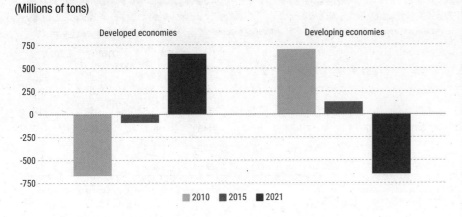

Developed economies   Developing economies

■ 2010 ■ 2015 ■ 2021

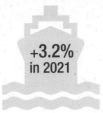

Seaborne trade
jumped by 3.2% in 2021

+3.2%
in 2021

64% of all goods **discharged** and **42%** of all goods **loaded** in **Asian** seaports

Developing
economies' **share**
of **seaborne** trade
imports **stood at 61%**
in 2021

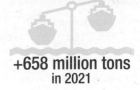

Developed
economies' **seaborne**
trade **balance** was

+658 million tons
in 2021

Table 5.1.1 | Total seaborne trade by group of economies

Group of economies	Loaded			Discharged			Balance	
	Volume		Annual growth rate	Volume		Annual growth rate	Volume	
	(Millions of tons)		(Percentage)	(Millions of tons)		(Percentage)	(Millions of tons)	
	2016	2021	2021	2016	2021	2021	2016	2021
World[a]	**10 247**	**10 985**	**3.2**	**10 303**	**10 975**	**3.2**	**-57**	**10**
Developed economies	4 500	4 936	2.4	4 553	4 278	4.1	-53	658
Developing economies	5 747	6 049	3.9	5 750	6 698	2.7	-4	-648
Developing economies: Africa	694	762	3.6	480	553	8.5	214	209
Developing economies: Americas	1 355	1 383	0.7	566	638	8.2	789	745
Developing economies: Asia and Oceania	3 698	3 904	5.1	4 704	5 507	1.5	-1 006	-1 603

[a] Annual world totals of goods loaded and discharged are not necessarily the same, given bilateral asymmetries in international merchandise trade statistics and that goods loaded in one calendar year may reach their port of destination in the next calendar year.

Table 5.1.2 | Seaborne trade by cargo type and group of economies

Crude oil

Group of economies	Loaded			Discharged			Balance	
	Volume		Annual growth rate	Volume		Annual growth rate	Volume	
	(Millions of tons)		(Percentage)	(Millions of tons)		(Percentage)	(Millions of tons)	
	2016	2021	2021	2016	2021	2021	2016	2021
World[a]	**1 832**	**1 700**	**-0.9**	**1 985**	**1 846**	**-1.0**	**-153**	**-146**
Developed economies	339	429	-2.3	1 104	879	0.1	-764	-450
Developing economies	1 493	1 272	-0.4	882	968	-1.9	611	304
Developing economies: Africa	271	226	-3.7	39	25	-19.0	233	202
Developing economies: Americas	232	190	-5.9	52	36	-6.7	181	154
Developing economies: Asia and Oceania	989	855	1.8	791	906	-1.1	198	-51

[a] Annual world totals of goods loaded and discharged are not necessarily the same, given bilateral asymmetries in international merchandise trade statistics and that goods loaded in one calendar year may reach their port of destination in the next calendar year.

Other tanker trade

Group of economies	Loaded			Discharged			Balance	
	Volume		Annual growth rate	Volume		Annual growth rate	Volume	
	(Millions of tons)		(Percentage)	(Millions of tons)		(Percentage)	(Millions of tons)	
	2016	2021	2021	2016	2021	2021	2016	2021
World[a]	**1 238**	**1 252**	**4.1**	**1 235**	**1 273**	**4.1**	**3**	**-21**
Developed economies	550	503	2.8	517	430	8.6	33	73
Developing economies	688	749	5.0	718	843	1.9	-30	-94
Developing economies: Africa	59	100	18.6	81	118	10.5	-22	-19
Developing economies: Americas	81	71	-5.6	128	129	-0.4	-47	-58
Developing economies: Asia and Oceania	548	579	4.4	509	596	0.8	40	-17

[a] Annual world totals of goods loaded and discharged are not necessarily the same, given bilateral asymmetries in international merchandise trade statistics and that goods loaded in one calendar year may reach their port of destination in the next calendar year.

Dry cargo

Group of economies	Loaded			Discharged			Balance	
	Volume		Annual growth rate	Volume		Annual growth rate	Volume	
	(Millions of tons)		(Percentage)	(Millions of tons)		(Percentage)	(Millions of tons)	
	2016	2021	2021	2016	2021	2021	2016	2021
World[a]	**7 176**	**8 033**	**4.0**	**7 083**	**7 856**	**4.1**	**93**	**177**
Developed economies	3 610	4 005	2.9	2 932	2 969	4.7	678	1 035
Developing economies	3 566	4 029	5.1	4 150	4 887	3.7	-585	-858
Developing economies: Africa	364	436	4.6	360	410	10.2	3	26
Developing economies: Americas	1 041	1 122	2.4	386	472	12.2	655	649
Developing economies: Asia and Oceania	2 161	2 471	6.4	3 405	4 004	2.2	-1 243	-1 534

[a] Annual world totals of goods loaded and discharged are not necessarily the same, given bilateral asymmetries in international merchandise trade statistics and that goods loaded in one calendar year may reach their port of destination in the next calendar year.

Table 5.1.3 | **Development of goods loaded worldwide by type of cargo**
(Millions of tons)

Year	Total goods	Crude oil	Other tanker trade	Dry cargo
1976	3 366	1 555	289	1 522
1981	3 555	1 364	327	1 864
1986	3 385	1 126	424	1 835
1991	4 120	1 333	457	2 330
1996	4 758	1 590	537	2 631
2001	6 020	1 678	499	3 844
2006	7 702	1 783	915	5 004
2011	8 739	1 751	1 028	5 959
2016	10 247	1 832	1 238	7 176
2021	10 985	1 700	1 252	8 033

5.2 Merchant fleet

Map 5.2 Building, ownership, registration and recycling of ships, 2021
(Percentage of world total)

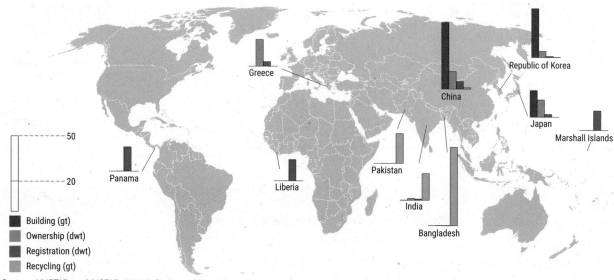

Sources: UNCTADstat (UNCTAD, 2022a), Clarksons Research.
Note: Top three countries in each segment are shown. Building and recycling are estimated deliveries and demolitions during 2021. Registration and ownership figures refer to the beginning of the year 2022.

Concepts and definitions

The unit dead-weight tons (dwt) is used to indicate the cargo carrying capacity of a ship, while gross tons (gt) reflect its size. The latter is relevant to measure shipbuilding and recycling activity, while the former is used to capture the capacity to transport cargo.

The presented statistics on fleet registration (the flag of a ship), shipbuilding and recycling cover all commercial ships of 100 gt and more. The market shares for ownership only cover larger ships of 1000 gt and above, as the true ownership is not always known for smaller vessels.

World fleet development and composition

In January 2022, the world fleet reached a carrying capacity of 2.2 billion dwt, 63 million dwt more than the previous year. Over recent years, tonnage has increased considerably in all segments except general cargo carriers. Bulk carriers recorded an especially rapid increase. Between 2012 and 2022, their share in total carrying capacity rose from 41 to 43 per cent, whereas the share of oil tankers shrank from 30 to 29 per cent, and the share of general cargo from 5 to 4 per cent.

Shipbuilding and recycling

In 2021, global shipbuilding was concentrated in China, the Republic of Korea and Japan. These three economies accounted for 94 per cent of shipbuilding in terms of gross tonnage. In ship recycling, Bangladesh and Pakistan jointly accounted for 72 per cent and India for an additional 18 per cent.

Figure 5.2.1 World fleet by principal vessel type
(Millions of dead-weight tons)

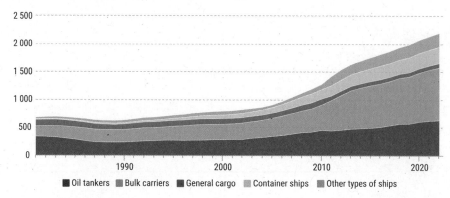

Sources: UNCTADstat (UNCTAD, 2022a); Clarksons Research.
Note: Commercial ships of 100 gt and above. Beginning-of-year figures.

Fleet ownership

As of January 2022, the top five ship-owning economies combined accounted for 53 per cent of world fleet tonnage. Greece held a market share of 18 per cent, followed by China (13 per cent), Japan (11 per cent), Singapore (6 per cent), and Hong Kong SAR (5 per cent). Half of the world's tonnage was owned by Asian companies. Owners from Europe accounted for 39 per cent and owners from Northern America for 6 per cent. Companies from Africa and from Latin America and the Caribbean had a share of just over one per cent each; Oceania just below one.

Figure 5.2.2 Fleet market by region of beneficial ownership, 2022
(Millions of dead-weight tons)

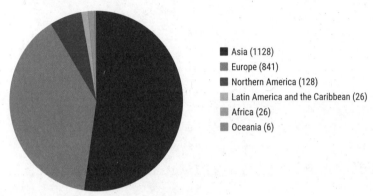

- Asia (1128)
- Europe (841)
- Northern America (128)
- Latin America and the Caribbean (26)
- Africa (26)
- Oceania (6)

Sources: UNCTADstat (UNCTAD, 2022a); Clarksons Research.
Note: Commercial ships of 1000 gt and above. Beginning-of-year figures.

Major flags of registration

Many commercial ships are registered under a flag that does not match the nationality of the vessel owner. For example, at the beginning of 2022, 49 per cent of all ships owned by Japanese entities were registered in Panama; of the ships owned by Greek entities, 25 per cent were registered in Liberia and another 23 per cent in the Marshall Islands.

Panama (350 million dwt), Liberia (335 million dwt) and the Marshall Islands (290 million dwt) represented the leading flags of registration. While the size of the register of Panama has remained almost unchanged over the last decade, the Marshall Islands and Liberia have caught up, with Liberia skyrocketing since 2018.

Figure 5.2.3 Vessels capacity in top five registries
(Millions of dead-weight tons)

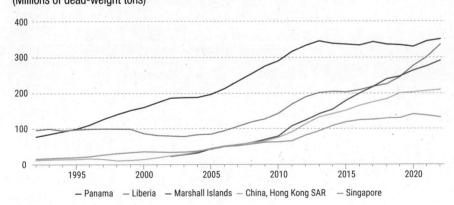

— Panama — Liberia — Marshall Islands — China, Hong Kong SAR — Singapore

Sources: UNCTADstat (UNCTAD, 2022a); Clarksons Research.
Note: Commercial ships of 100 gt and above. Beginning-of-year figures. Ranked by the values as of 1 January 2022.

World commercial fleet **grew** by **63 million dwt**

between January 2021 and January 2022

94% of global **shipbuilding** occurred in **China**, the **Republic of Korea** and **Japan** in 2021

Half of the world fleet **owned** by **Asian companies**

Of the world's 2.2 billion dwt of **carrying capacity, 1.0 billion** was registered in

Panama   Liberia   Marshall Islands
in January 2022

Table 5.2.1 | Merchant fleet registration by group of economies

Group of economies	2017				2022			
	Tonnage		Vessels		Tonnage		Vessels	
	(Millions of dwt)	Share in world (Percentage)	(Thousands)	Share in world (Percentage)	(Millions of dwt)	Share in world (Percentage)	(Thousands)	Share in world (Percentage)
World	**1 868**	**100.0**	**94**	**100.0**	**2 199**	**100.0**	**103**	**100.0**
Developed economies	455	24.3	31	32.7	466	21.2	32	30.7
Developing economies	1 409	75.4	61	65.6	1 727	78.5	70	67.6
Developing economies: Africa	235	12.6	7	7.1	365	16.6	8	8.2
Developing economies: Americas	463	24.8	16	17.2	463	21.0	16	15.7
Developing economies: Asia and Oceania	712	38.1	39	41.3	899	40.9	45	43.7
Selected groups								
Developing economies excluding China	1 329	71.2	57	60.8	1 612	73.3	62	60.5
Developing economies excluding LDCs	1 180	63.1	55	59.2	1 371	62.3	62	60.3
LDCs	229	12.3	6	6.4	356	16.2	7	7.3
LLDCs	4	0.2	1	1.1	3	0.1	1	1.1
SIDS (UN-OHRLLS)	471	25.2	14	15.0	543	24.7	14	14.1
HIPCs (IMF)	225	12.0	6	5.9	352	16.0	7	6.8
BRICS	110	5.9	10	10.3	149	6.8	13	12.7
G20	554	29.6	47	49.8	620	28.2	52	50.9

Sources: UNCTADstat (UNCTAD, 2022a); Clarksons Research.
Note: Commercial ships of 100 gt and above. Figures refer to the beginning of the year.

Table 5.2.2 | Fleet ownership and registration, main economies, 1 January 2022

Vessels
(Number of vessels)

Economy of ownership (Ranked by number of ships owned)	Flag of registration (Ranked by number of ships registered)							
	Panama	China	Liberia	Marshall Islands	Singapore	Indonesia	China, Hong Kong SAR	World
China	728	5 357	209	149	60	6	945	8 007
Greece	450	0	1 214	1 108	25	2	17	4 870
Japan	1 976	0	268	261	181	7	49	4 007
Singapore	289	5	290	147	1 371	89	116	2 799
Indonesia	26	3	8	18	17	2 283	1	2 411
Germany	34	0	510	83	81	0	17	2 221
Norway	43	0	82	122	84	4	47	1 987
Russian Federation	33	0	109	0	2	0	2	1 833
China, Hong Kong SAR	373	24	71	79	43	4	861	1 822
United States of America	62	1	95	326	7	0	32	1 785
World	**6 681**	**5 420**	**4 266**	**3 955**	**2 456**	**2 445**	**2 375**	55 037

Sources: UNCTADstat (UNCTAD, 2022a); Clarksons Research.
Note: Commercial ships of 1000 gt and above.

Tonnage
(Thousands of dead-weight tons)

Economy of ownership (Ranked by tonnage owned)	Flag of registration (Ranked by tonnage registered)							
	Panama	Liberia	Marshall Islands	China, Hong Kong SAR	Singapore	Malta	China	World
Greece	25 073	106 897	82 885	1 073	1 261	63 015	0	384 430
China	31 518	18 157	9 840	86 959	4 687	3 420	113 036	277 843
Japan	127 509	25 214	16 065	2 719	10 647	1 207	0	236 638
Singapore	13 089	23 100	9 090	6 441	67 869	3 160	980	136 244
China, Hong Kong SAR	16 811	7 207	4 616	72 061	4 540	1 085	166	111 588
Korea, Republic of	42 792	4 359	27 142	986	274	305	2	92 302
Germany	835	29 410	4 662	1 282	4 247	4 062	0	79 593
Bermuda	1 235	7 546	23 006	8 166	1 247	102	0	63 407
Norway	1 724	4 572	7 305	8 609	4 611	1 015	0	59 931
United Kingdom	3 461	19 777	9 913	323	325	4 881	0	58 747
World	**349 802**	**335 098**	**289 757**	**207 731**	**131 138**	**114 876**	**114 357**	2 180 058

Sources: UNCTADstat (UNCTAD, 2022a); Clarksons Research.
Note: Commercial ships of 1000 gt and above.

5.3 Maritime transport indicators

Map 5.3 Liner shipping connectivity, 2021–2022

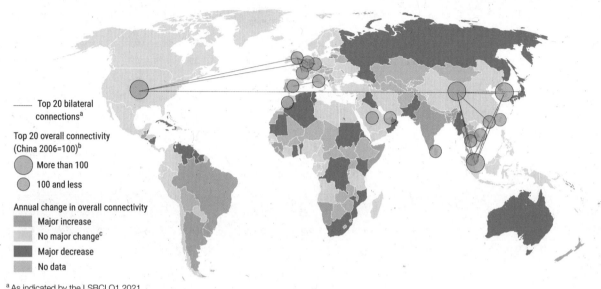

- —— Top 20 bilateral connections[a]

Top 20 overall connectivity (China 2006=100)[b]
- ⬤ More than 100
- ⬤ 100 and less

Annual change in overall connectivity
- ▨ Major increase
- ▨ No major change[c]
- ▨ Major decrease
- ▨ No data

[a] As indicated by the LSBCI Q1 2021.
[b] As indicated by the LSCI Q1 2022.
[c] Change of less than 5 per cent, year-on-year.

Concepts and definitions

The liner shipping connectivity index (LSCI) indicates a country's position within global liner shipping networks. It is calculated from the number of ship calls, their container carrying capacity, the number of services and companies, the size of the largest ship, and the number of other countries connected through direct liner shipping services.

The liner shipping bilateral connectivity index (LSBCI) is calculated from five components, including the number of transshipments required to trade and the connections available using one transshipment.

Port container traffic is measured in twenty-foot equivalent units (TEUs). One TEU represents the volume of a standard 20-feet long intermodal container.

The number of port calls and the time spent in ports are derived from combining automatic identification system data with port mapping intelligence. These data cover ships of 1000 gt and above.

Liner shipping connectivity throughout the world

In the third quarter of 2022, China was the economy best connected to the global liner shipping network, as measured by the LSCI. The Republic of Korea, Singapore, Malaysia and the United States of America followed next in the rankings. Regional leaders included: Spain and the Netherlands in Europe; Panama and Colombia in Latin America and the Caribbean; Morocco and Egypt in Africa; and Sri Lanka and India in Southern Asia. Among the least connected 30 economies, 18 are SIDS, four of which are also LDCs. An additional three are coastal LDCs.

In 2021, 17 of the top 20 bilateral connections were intra-regional within Europe or within Eastern and South-Eastern Asia. The only inter-regional connections among the top 20 were between the United States of America and highly connected economies in the regions mentioned above: China in Asia as well as the Netherlands and the United Kingdom in Europe.

Figure 5.3.1 Liner shipping connectivity index, top five economies
(China Q1 2006=100)

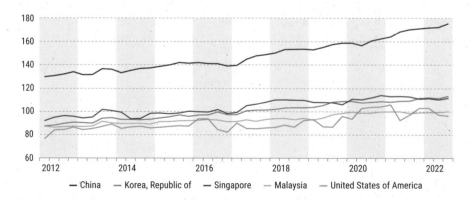

— China   — Korea, Republic of   — Singapore   — Malaysia   — United States of America

Port container traffic

In 2020, 798.9 million TEUs of containers were handled in ports worldwide. World container port throughput declined by 1.0 per cent between 2019 and 2020. This reduction was moderate in comparison to other shipping market segments and total seaborne trade (see section 5.1). It reflected the resilience of containerized trade amid the disruption caused by the COVID-19 pandemic.

Figure 5.3.2 World container port throughput
(Millions of twenty-foot equivalent units)

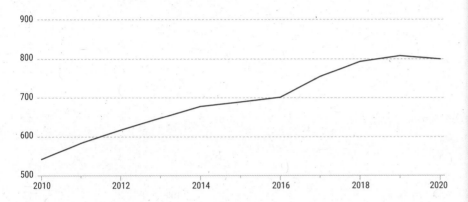

Asia's leading role as a global maritime freight loading and discharging centre (see section 5.1) and its high liner shipping connectivity is mirrored in the region's high contribution to containerized port throughput. In 2020, ports in developing economies of Asia and Oceania handled 62 per cent of the world port container traffic. The shares of the developing Americas and developing Africa were significantly lower, at less than 7 per cent each.

Port calls

Globally, 4.3 million port calls were recorded in 2021. The economy that recorded most port calls of ships in 2021 was Norway. As a median, cargo-carrying ships left Norwegian ports 10 hours after their arrival.[1]

[1] For further analyses on maritime transport, see UNCTAD (2022d).

Figure 5.3.3 Containerized port traffic by group of economies, 2020
(Millions of twenty-foot equivalent units)

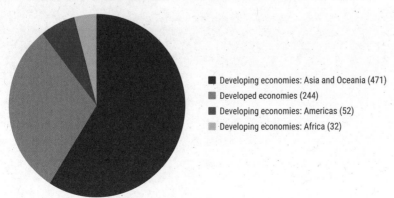

- Developing economies: Asia and Oceania (471)
- Developed economies (244)
- Developing economies: Americas (52)
- Developing economies: Africa (32)

China, Singapore and the **Republic of Korea** – the economies **most integrated** into global liner **shipping networks**

Bilateral **connectivity higher within** than between **continents**

Developing economies in **Asia and Oceania** handled **62%** of world port **container traffic** in 2020

In **Norway, cargo ships stay** on average only **10 hours** at port

Table 5.3.1 **Liner shipping connectivity index of most connected economies, by region**
(China Q1 2006 = 100)

	Economy (Ranked by Q3 2022 value)	Q1 2011	Q1 2016	Q1 2021	Q1 2022	Q2 2022	Q3 2022
Northern America and Europe	1. United States of America	78	93	106	103	103	96
	2. Spain	74	82	90	90	90	91
	3. Netherlands	81	83	92	91	91	91
	4. United Kingdom	81	86	91	90	90	89
	5. Belgium	80	86	88	87	87	88
Latin America and the Caribbean	1. Panama	37	50	50	51	51	50
	2. Colombia	33	49	49	48	48	48
	3. Mexico	37	47	49	48	48	47
	4. Brazil	32	35	36	40	40	40
	5. Peru	26	32	39	39	39	40
Africa	1. Morocco	51	58	69	69	69	71
	2. Egypt	47	59	68	67	67	68
	3. South Africa	37	39	41	39	39	40
	4. Ghana	21	22	40	36	36	37
	5. Togo	16	31	37	36	36	37
Asia	1. China	131	142	164	172	172	175
	2. Korea, Republic of	86	97	108	112	112	113
	3. Singapore	94	100	113	111	111	111
	4. Malaysia	80	92	100	99	99	100
	5. China, Hong Kong SAR	96	90	94	87	87	85
Oceania	1. Australia	31	33	38	36	36	36
	2. New Zealand	20	21	29	31	31	31
	3. Papua New Guinea	8	10	11	11	11	11
	4. New Caledonia	12	12	11	10	10	11
	5. Fiji	12	11	9	10	10	11

Table 5.3.2 | **Time at port, by market segment, in the top 20 economies by port call, 2021**

	Number of port calls	Median time at port (days)						
		All market segments	Liquid bulk	Container ship	Dry breakbulk	Dry bulk	LPG carriers	LNG carriers
Norway	696 827	0.4	0.6	0.4	0.3	0.8	0.8	0.3
Japan	272 723	0.4	0.3	0.4	1.2	0.8	0.3	1.0
China	260 464	1.1	1.1	0.7	1.5	2.0	1.0	1.2
United States of America[a]	260 187	1.6	1.6	1.2	2.0	2.2	1.8	1.3
Italy	230 097	1.3	1.3	1.0	2.0	3.5	1.6	..
Türkiye	204 553	1.2	1.2	0.6	1.5	3.9	1.2	1.2
Indonesia	181 658	1.3	1.3	1.1	1.2	2.8	1.1	1.4
United Kingdom[b]	174 726	1.2	1.0	0.8	1.5	3.0	1.1	1.2
Greece	153 559	0.8	0.6	1.0	1.1	0.6	1.0	1.2
Netherlands	121 650	0.6	0.6	0.9	0.4	1.2	1.0	1.0
Spain	118 511	0.9	0.9	0.7	1.2	1.8	1.0	1.0
Canada	111 934	0.7	1.1	1.8	0.8	0.3	1.5	..
Denmark	106 560	0.8	0.7	0.5	0.9	0.8	1.1	..
Germany	95 586	0.8	0.6	1.1	0.9	2.5	0.9	..
Korea, Republic of	94 594	0.9	0.8	0.7	1.2	2.1	0.8	1.0
Croatia	73 290	1.2	0.9	0.6	2.5	2.5	..	1.6
Sweden	67 288	0.8	0.7	0.7	1.0	0.5	0.8	0.7
France[c]	66 103	1.2	1.0	1.0	1.6	3.0	1.1	1.1
Russian Federation	64 406	1.5	1.1	1.6	1.8	2.5	1.5	1.1
Australia	54 859	1.6	1.3	1.6	2.0	1.7	0.9	1.3
World	**4 286 204**	1.0	1.0	0.8	1.2	2.1	1.0	1.1

Note: Economies are ranked by number of port calls. Number of port calls includes arrivals of ferries, roll-on roll-off and passenger ships, for which the time in port is not computed.
[a] Excluding Puerto Rico and United States Virgin Islands.
[b] United Kingdom of Great Britain and Northern Ireland excluding Channel Islands and Isle of Man.
[c] Excluding French Guiana, Guadeloupe, Martinique, Mayotte, Monaco and Reunion.

Table 5.3.3 | **Liner shipping connectivity of the world's seven most connected economies**

Economy (Ranked by LSCI 2021)	Year	LSCI (China Q1 2006=100)	LSBCI vis-à-vis ...						
			China	Singapore	Korea, Rep. of	United States of America	Malaysia	China, Hong Kong SAR	Netherlands
China	2016	142	–	0.554	0.622	0.552	0.562	0.563	0.469
	2021	164	–	0.568	0.634	0.556	0.578	0.551	0.474
Singapore	2016	100		–	0.501	0.420	0.580	0.504	0.443
	2021	113		–	0.521	0.443	0.588	0.502	0.467
Korea, Republic of	2016	97			–	0.432	0.504	0.517	0.441
	2021	108			–	0.461	0.505	0.462	0.460
United States of America	2016	93				–	0.393	0.447	0.442
	2021	106				–	0.463	0.456	0.506
Malaysia	2016	92					–	0.507	0.429
	2021	100					–	0.488	0.439
China, Hong Kong SAR	2016	90						–	0.429
	2021	94						–	0.445
Netherlands	2016	83							–
	2021	92							–

Note: All index values refer to the value at Q1 of the indicated year.

ANNEXES

6.1 Key indicators by economy, 2021

Economy	Merchandise trade			Trade in services		GDP	
	Exports	Imports	Terms of trade	Exports	Imports	Per capita (nominal)	Growth (real)[a]
	(Millions of US$)	(Millions of US$)	(2015=100)	(Millions of US$)	(Millions of US$)	(US$)	(Percentage)
World	**22 328 177**	**22 586 618**	**103**	**6 071 633**	**5 623 458**	**12 170**	**5.7**
Developed economies	12 410 429	13 319 230	101	4 420 647	3 768 053	43 149	5.0
Albania	3 559	7 718	104	4 094	1 996	6 129	5.5
Andorra	(e) 148	(e) 1 823	93	..	..	38 488	0.5
Australia	344 829	261 165	164	(e) 45 274	(e) 39 272	66 209	4.6
Austria	202 806	219 520	96	70 210	66 987	53 301	4.2
Belarus	39 762	41 387	98	10 234	5 672	6 992	2.3
Belgium	545 284	510 208	99	136 653	134 494	50 848	4.7
Bermuda	12	1 085	157	(e) 1 058	(e) 832	126 972	4.2
Bosnia and Herzegovina	8 614	13 029	112	2 250	693	6 677	3.9
Bulgaria	41 018	46 195	102	10 971	5 656	11 553	3.3
Canada	507 615	504 017	111	(e) 103 790	(e) 104 903	52 140	4.6
Croatia	22 812	34 588	96	16 770	5 163	16 103	6.5
Cyprus	3 787	10 168	86	18 212	12 839	29 883	3.0
Czechia	226 407	211 508	99	29 706	24 624	26 968	3.5
Denmark	125 945	120 307	99	93 382	81 723	67 348	3.8
Estonia	21 518	23 609	101	9 943	8 259	26 889	6.8
Faroe Islands	1 600	1 477	98	-	-	..	..
Finland	81 971	85 975	95	32 935	35 696	53 252	2.8
France	584 768	714 102	96	303 028	258 299	44 028	7.0
Germany	1 631 931	1 420 129	99	(e) 377 236	(e) 381 033	50 687	2.9
Gibraltar	(e) 150	(e) 840	79	-	-	..	..
Greece	47 170	75 855	96	41 397	26 033	20 246	6.0
Greenland	774	858	99	-	-	59 066	1.9
Holy See	..	..	..	..	..	..	..
Hungary	141 921	141 973	104	26 088	20 199	18 619	6.7
Iceland	5 987	7 817	99	3 708	2 952	68 448	3.5
Ireland	190 319	119 496	88	337 759	341 456	97 753	10.9
Israel	60 159	92 155	90	(e) 71 785	(e) 32 073	52 666	5.3
Italy	610 284	557 524	99	102 421	113 497	35 366	6.6
Japan	756 032	768 976	95	(e) 167 851	(e) 207 337	39 749	1.6
Korea, Republic of	644 400	615 093	92	(e) 122 741	(e) 127 120	34 700	4.0
Latvia	20 823	24 447	105	5 697	3 622	20 734	4.3
Lithuania	40 828	44 585	98	15 214	9 061	23 417	4.7
Luxembourg	16 623	25 811	95	140 047	110 508	132 918	4.8
Malta	3 111	6 656	104	18 095	14 680	31 082	4.3
Moldova, Republic of	3 144	7 177	108	1 635	1 177	4 315	6.5
Montenegro	515	2 956	..	1 881	755	9 027	9.5
Netherlands	836 512	757 986	97	(e) 247 556	(e) 236 765	57 510	3.9
New Zealand	44 758	49 855	115	(e) 9 378	(e) 13 356	45 866	-0.5

| Current account balance | FDI | | CPI growth | Population | | | Fleet size[b] | Economy |
	Outflows	Inflows		Total	Share of urban	Old-age dependency ratio		
(Millions of US$)	(Millions of US$)	(Millions of US$)	(Percentage)	(Thousands)	(Percentage)	(Percentage)	(1000 of dwt)	
709 935	**1 707 594**	**1 582 310**	**4.8**	**7 909 295**	**56.5**	**14.8**	**2 199 107**	**World**
230 420	1 269 212	745 739	3.4	1 343 447	79.5	30.1	465 687	Developed economies
-1 393	63	1 234	2.0	2 855	63.0	24.1	47	Albania
..	..	..	1.7	79	87.9	20.1	..	Andorra
56 691	9 224	25 085	2.8	25 921	86.4	25.5	2 421	Australia
-2 541	10 781	5 823	2.8	8 922	59.0	29.4	0	Austria
1 843	-85	1 233	9.5	9 578	79.9	25.4	1	Belarus
-2 157	45 624	25 577	3.2	11 611	98.1	30.4	9 791	Belgium
(e) 765	-25	1	1.3	64	100.0	30.1	7 888	Bermuda
-485	38	519	2.0	3 271	49.4	27.1	..	Bosnia and Herzegovina
-257	150	1 496	2.8	6 886	76.0	35.3	133	Bulgaria
827	89 874	59 676	3.4	38 155	81.7	28.2	3 269	Canada
2 251	122	569	2.6	4 060	57.9	34.4	1 531	Croatia
-2 031	-3 329	463	2.2	900	66.9	20.8	33 461	Cyprus
-2 282	5 583	5 806	3.8	10 511	74.2	32.2	..	Czechia
32 957	22 399	5 541	1.9	5 854	88.2	31.9	26 147	Denmark
-624	1 547	989	4.5	1 329	69.4	32.3	81	Estonia
..	..	..	..	53	42.6	29.1	365	Faroe Islands
2 722	4 092	9 393	2.1	5 536	85.6	37.1	1 260	Finland
10 598	-2 839	14 193	(e) 2.1	66 913	81.5	34.3	8 377	France
314 087	151 690	31 267	3.2	83 409	77.5	34.7	7 096	Germany
..	..	..	..	33	100.0	32.7	1 417	Gibraltar
-12 721	926	5 732	0.6	10 445	80.0	35.5	61 817	Greece
..	..	..	0.0	56	87.5	13.6	1	Greenland
..	..	..	..	1	100.0	-	..	Holy See
-5 243	2 882	5 459	5.1	9 710	72.2	31.4	0	Hungary
-699	19	174	4.5	370	93.9	22.5	16	Iceland
69 541	61 979	15 702	2.4	4 987	63.9	22.7	382	Ireland
20 979	9 713	29 615	1.5	8 900	92.7	19.9	449	Israel
53 095	11 759	8 487	1.9	59 240	71.3	37.2	9 969	Italy
142 491	146 782	24 652	-0.3	124 613	91.9	51.0	40 263	Japan
88 302	60 820	16 820	2.5	51 830	81.4	23.3	15 635	Korea, Republic of
-1 133	3 361	5 325	3.2	1 874	68.4	34.4	162	Latvia
937	663	2 053	4.6	2 787	68.2	32.1	213	Lithuania
4 322	25 398	-9 054	3.5	639	91.7	21.3	1 401	Luxembourg
-1 010	7 247	4 005	0.7	527	94.8	27.7	114 910	Malta
-1 590	25	264	5.1	3 062	43.0	20.4	462	Moldova, Republic of
-538	11	664	2.4	628	67.8	24.8	143	Montenegro
96 623	28 861	-81 056	2.8	17 502	92.6	30.9	6 661	Netherlands
-14 268	-1 876	3 482	3.9	5 130	86.8	24.4	207	New Zealand

Economy	Merchandise trade			Trade in services		GDP	
	Exports	Imports	Terms of trade	Exports	Imports	Per capita (nominal)	Growth (real)[a]
	(Millions of US$)	(Millions of US$)	(2015=100)	(Millions of US$)	(Millions of US$)	(US$)	(Percentage)
North Macedonia	8 186	11 386	88	2 058	1 460	6 680	4.0
Norway	160 106	97 764	113	40 301	41 362	88 792	3.3
Poland	337 908	338 341	98	80 572	49 339	17 443	4.8
Portugal	75 181	97 713	98	32 000	20 807	24 277	4.8
Romania	87 384	116 228	99	33 015	21 699	14 560	5.5
Russian Federation	493 820	303 994	115	(e) 56 587	(e) 75 902	12 197	4.7
Saint Pierre and Miquelon	5	118	91	-	-	..	..
San Marino	..	..	..	..	..	51 256	5.7
Serbia	25 564	33 797	97	11 515	8 556	8 050	7.3
Slovakia	103 557	103 499	102	11 187	10 246	21 093	3.0
Slovenia	57 352	57 560	101	9 763	6 930	28 261	5.3
Spain	382 993	418 176	98	119 046	73 053	29 820	4.5
Sweden	189 734	186 899	100	79 036	79 962	59 411	4.0
Switzerland, Liechtenstein	380 194	324 069	105	134 785	142 347	93 645	3.3
Ukraine	68 075	72 527	128	18 631	14 342	-	3.1
United Kingdom	468 177	693 774	95	417 545	242 926	47 337	7.5
United States of America	1 754 300	2 935 314	105	795 273	550 025	67 904	5.7
Developing economies	9 917 748	9 267 388	103	1 650 986	1 855 405	5 831	6.7
Developing economies: Africa	560 664	628 831	124	100 483	159 525	1 915	5.0
Algeria	(e) 36 700	(e) 36 000	116	(e) 3 025	(e) 6 664	3 747	4.4
Angola	33 581	11 795	112	94	7 050	2 294	0.0
Benin	3 445	4 333	116	(e) 555	(e) 984	1 276	4.5
Botswana	7 206	8 359	86	(e) 468	(e) 1 127	6 772	4.8
Burkina Faso	5 043	4 614	121	(e) 573	(e) 1 508	847	4.8
Burundi	156	1 030	117	-	-	292	2.7
Cabo Verde	54	800	96	282	229	3 214	3.8
Cameroon	(e) 4 100	(e) 6 100	133	-	-	1 609	3.0
Central African Republic	(e) 162	(e) 590	93	-	-	456	0.0
Chad	(e) 2 560	(e) 2 745	119	(e) 223	(e) 2 054	733	1.5
Comoros	34	328	60	(e) 51	(e) 114	1 593	2.0
Congo	(e) 6 970	(e) 2 302	126	-	-	2 124	-1.6
Congo, Dem. Rep. of the	(e) 23 500	(e) 10 300	133	-	-	534	3.5
Côte d'Ivoire	14 994	14 007	94	(e) 871	(e) 3 648	2 517	6.0
Djibouti	(e) 3 280	(e) 4 011	102	-	-	3 293	5.1
Egypt	43 626	83 503	124	(e) 21 897	(e) 22 951	3 715	4.1
Equatorial Guinea	(e) 5 700	(e) 1 900	151	-	-	8 208	1.9
Eritrea	(e) 600	(e) 1 154	106	-	-	619	1.5
Eswatini	2 060	1 936	106	(e) 64	(e) 228	3 725	1.4
Ethiopia	3 949	15 973	105	(e) 5 578	(e) 6 654	800	3.2
French Southern Territories	..	..	..	..	..	..	..
Gabon	(e) 5 962	(e) 3 444	120	-	-	8 117	1.5
Gambia	32	607	97	104	119	763	4.8
Ghana	14 727	13 629	123	(e) 9 174	(e) 12 338	2 321	4.1
Guinea	(e) 10 433	(e) 4 094	135	27	1 166	1 314	5.2

| Current account balance | FDI | | CPI growth | Population | | | Fleet size[b] | Economy |
	Outflows	Inflows		Total	Share of urban	Old-age dependency ratio		
(Millions of US$)	(Millions of US$)	(Millions of US$)	(Percentage)	(Thousands)	(Percentage)	(Percentage)	(1000 of dwt)	
-479	91	606	3.2	2 103	58.8	21.4	..	North Macedonia
71 551	1 382	-1 628	3.5	5 403	83.3	27.9	23 605	Norway
-3 895	178	24 816	5.1	38 308	60.1	28.6	102	Poland
-2 848	-1 441	8 020	0.9	10 290	66.8	35.2	25 968	Portugal
-19 751	-31	8 610	5.0	19 329	54.3	29.1	80	Romania
122 040	63 602	38 240	6.7	145 103	74.9	23.4	11 039	Russian Federation
..	..	..	..	6	90.3	25.9	..	Saint Pierre and Miquelon
..	..	..	2.1	34	97.6	30.0	..	San Marino
-2 742	392	5 060	4.1	8 959	56.7	28.5	..	Serbia
-2 220	389	59	2.8	5 448	53.8	25.8	..	Slovakia
2 073	922	1 517	1.9	2 119	55.4	31.9	3	Slovenia
13 263	-1 625	9 777	3.1	47 487	81.1	30.2	1 906	Spain
34 684	20 347	26 973	2.7	10 467	88.2	32.3	1 201	Sweden
75 502	-19 120	1 016	0.6	8 730	73.7	28.7	930	Switzerland, Liechtenstein
-2 639	-198	6 549	9.4	43 531	69.8	25.8	394	Ukraine
-82 534	107 741	27 561	2.6	67 538	84.0	29.8	31 953	United Kingdom
-821 645	403 101	367 376	4.7	340 354	83.0	25.7	12 528	United States of America
479 515	438 382	836 571	6.9	6 565 504	51.8	11.7	1 726 903	Developing economies
-41 438	2 653	82 991	22.7	1 392 394	44.0	6.2	365 235	Developing economies: Africa
(e) -3 444	-52	870	7.2	44 178	74.3	9.8	652	Algeria
8 399	-1 057	-4 150	25.8	34 504	67.5	5.0	322	Angola
(e) -534	28	242	1.7	12 997	49.0	5.7	2	Benin
(e) -82	-53	55	6.7	2 588	71.6	5.7	..	Botswana
(e) -271	26	137	3.9	22 101	31.2	4.8	..	Burkina Faso
(e) -488	1	8	8.3	12 551	14.1	4.8	..	Burundi
-254	-7	118	1.9	588	67.1	8.0	46	Cabo Verde
(e) -1 251	105	850	2.3	27 199	58.1	4.9	4 678	Cameroon
(e) -178	..	30	4.3	5 457	42.6	5.1	..	Central African Republic
(e) -904	..	562	-0.8	17 180	23.8	4.0	..	Chad
(e) -26	..	4	1.5	822	29.6	7.5	1 335	Comoros
(e) 469	25	3 691	2.0	5 836	68.3	4.8	6	Congo
(e) -547	192	1 870	9.0	95 894	46.2	5.9	40	Congo, Dem. Rep. of the
(e) -3 029	490	1 382	4.2	27 478	52.2	4.3	3	Côte d'Ivoire
(e) -36	..	167	1.2	1 106	78.2	6.9	3 155	Djibouti
(e) -18 436	367	5 122	4.5	109 262	42.9	7.7	1 725	Egypt
(e) -262	..	491	-0.1	1 634	73.6	5.4	66	Equatorial Guinea
(e) -265	..	70	4.5	3 620	42.0	7.1	14	Eritrea
(e) 25	59	126	3.7	1 192	24.4	6.5	..	Eswatini
(e) -3 169	..	4 259	26.8	120 283	22.2	5.5	338	Ethiopia
..	..	..	..	..	..	..	0	French Southern Territories
(e) -1 324	..	1 635	1.1	2 341	90.4	6.5	1 455	Gabon
-94	-3	252	7.4	2 640	63.2	4.5	7	Gambia
(e) -2 506	192	2 614	10.0	32 833	58.0	5.9	44	Ghana
4 639	-4	173	12.6	13 532	37.3	6.1	2	Guinea

Economy	Merchandise trade			Trade in services		GDP	
	Exports	Imports	Terms of trade	Exports	Imports	Per capita (nominal)	Growth (real)[a]
	(Millions of US$)	(Millions of US$)	(2015=100)	(Millions of US$)	(Millions of US$)	(US$)	(Percentage)
Guinea-Bissau	215	355	104	(e) 21	(e) 148	698	2.6
Kenya	6 739	19 559	92	(e) 4 628	(e) 4 008	2 019	4.7
Lesotho	1 064	(e) 2 051	78	19	407	1 224	3.6
Liberia	879	1 478	142	(e) 4	(e) 288	541	2.9
Libya	28 986	18 972	106	-	-	6 992	168.0
Madagascar	2 726	4 408	82	(e) 589	(e) 1 180	488	3.4
Malawi	(e) 1 007	(e) 3 257	90	-	-	609	2.5
Mali	5 015	6 530	124	(e) 513	(e) 2 343	868	3.0
Mauritania	(e) 4 343	(e) 3 564	152	(e) 193	(e) 782	1 994	3.1
Mauritius	1 964	5 142	94	1 233	1 430	8 518	3.8
Morocco	35 843	58 034	89	15 461	8 526	3 513	6.2
Mozambique	(e) 5 579	(e) 8 621	129	(e) 761	(e) 2 478	502	2.1
Namibia	(e) 6 696	(e) 9 122	104	413	589	4 981	2.1
Niger	1 211	2 741	105	(e) 164	(e) 1 029	611	4.6
Nigeria	46 932	51 941	127	(e) 4 082	(e) 15 165	2 151	3.0
Rwanda	1 530	2 895	119	(e) 579	(e) 666	784	4.5
Saint Helena	(e) 89	(e) 40	109	..	..	..	..
Sao Tome and Principe	21	166	91	(e) 57	(e) 50	2 313	2.5
Senegal	5 202	9 699	104	(e) 1 076	(e) 3 051	1 630	6.0
Seychelles	464	1 133	102	(e) 892	(e) 476	11 684	4.2
Sierra Leone	697	1 803	121	(e) 49	(e) 205	479	2.9
Somalia	(e) 450	(e) 1 220	122	-	-	115	1.1
South Africa	123 572	(e) 113 989	128	9 103	13 587	6 341	4.9
South Sudan	486	1 109	..	(e) 158	(e) 2 452	1 114	2.0
Sudan	4 279	9 238	100	(e) 1 880	(e) 1 391	569	0.1
Tanzania, United Republic of	6 391	10 024	117	(e) 3 228	(e) 1 719	1 138	4.7
Togo	1 350	2 632	102	(e) 612	(e) 464	911	4.3
Tunisia	16 689	22 488	91	(e) 2 718	(e) 2 583	3 525	3.9
Uganda	(e) 4 193	(e) 8 784	108	(e) 1 852	(e) 3 211	929	3.9
Western Sahara	..	..	..	..	..	..	..
Zambia	11 141	7 096	122	501	1 278	1 037	1.5
Zimbabwe	6 035	7 188	98	(e) 240	(e) 945	-	6.3
Developing economies: Americas	1 208 396	1 266 852	111	157 627	197 664	7 888	6.2
Anguilla	(e) 14	(e) 265	89	126	111	18 292	8.8
Antigua and Barbuda	19	596	94	713	337	15 318	2.5
Argentina	77 935	63 185	114	9 359	12 835	10 616	10.1
Aruba	128	1 053	95	2 073	932	25 979	7.0
Bahamas	565	3 201	95	(e) 2 995	(e) 1 655	26 742	3.5
Barbados	350	1 672	93	(e) 1 052	(e) 473	16 572	2.2
Belize	424	1 061	118	618	297	4 229	3.3
Bolivia (Plurinational State of)	11 030	9 559	131	407	1 991	3 176	3.3
Bonaire, Sint Eustatius and Saba	(e) 1	(e) 105	..	..	..	..	..
Brazil	280 815	234 690	123	33 164	50 275	7 487	4.6
British Virgin Islands	(e) 17	(e) 238	100	-	-	53 115	7.3

| Current account balance | FDI | | CPI growth | Population | | | Fleet size[b] | Economy |
| | Outflows | Inflows | | Total | Share of urban | Old-age dependency ratio | | |
(Millions of US$)	(Millions of US$)	(Millions of US$)	(Percentage)	(Thousands)	(Percentage)	(Percentage)	(1000 of dwt)	
(e) -91	0	24	3.3	2 061	44.6	5.0	2	Guinea-Bissau
(e) -6 057	-35	448	6.1	53 006	28.5	4.8	12	Kenya
-102	..	27	6.0	2 281	29.5	6.8	..	Lesotho
..	91	46	7.8	5 193	52.6	6.0	335 114	Liberia
(e) 6 987	-55	..	3.7	6 735	81.0	7.3	1 625	Libya
(e) -861	115	300	5.8	28 916	39.2	5.8	10	Madagascar
(e) -1 471	-21	50	9.3	19 890	17.7	5.0	..	Malawi
(e) -856	40	660	4.0	21 905	44.7	4.9	..	Mali
(e) -695	5	22	3.4	4 615	56.1	6.0	4	Mauritania
-1 527	86	253	4.0	1 299	40.8	17.3	149	Mauritius
-3 261	506	2 153	1.4	37 077	64.1	11.3	156	Morocco
(e) -3 653	194	5 102	5.7	32 077	37.6	4.8	31	Mozambique
-1 120	17	412	3.6	2 530	53.0	6.7	56	Namibia
(e) -1 737	58	755	3.8	25 253	16.8	5.0	5	Niger
(e) -3 712	1 237	4 844	17.0	213 401	52.7	5.5	4 966	Nigeria
(e) -1 208	..	212	0.8	13 462	17.6	5.4	..	Rwanda
..	..	..	..	5	40.2	45.1	..	Saint Helena
(e) -50	0	60	8.1	223	75.1	6.7	689	Sao Tome and Principe
(e) -2 815	217	2 232	2.2	16 877	48.6	5.7	17	Senegal
0	-3	157	9.8	106	58.0	11.4	208	Seychelles
(e) -520	..	218	11.9	8 421	43.4	5.5	2 928	Sierra Leone
..	..	456	..	17 066	46.7	5.2	1	Somalia
15 529	19	40 889	4.5	59 392	67.8	9.1	540	South Africa
(e) -392	..	68	5.3	10 748	20.5	5.4	..	South Sudan
(e) -2 970	..	462	359.1	45 657	35.6	6.2	6	Sudan
(e) -2 445	..	922	3.7	63 588	36.0	5.9	1 900	Tanzania, United Republic of
(e) -10	225	130	4.3	8 645	43.4	5.5	2 604	Togo
(e) -3 224	47	660	5.7	12 263	69.9	13.3	320	Tunisia
(e) -3 468	0	1 142	2.2	45 854	25.6	3.2	..	Uganda
..	..	..	..	566	86.9	8.0	..	Western Sahara
2 352	-453	-457	20.5	19 473	45.2	3.2	3	Zambia
-	55	166	98.5	15 994	32.3	6.0	..	Zimbabwe
-76 988	41 770	134 458	15.0	651 680	81.3	13.2	462 760	Developing economies: Americas
-146	-5	81	2.4	16	100.0	14.1	4	Anguilla
-221	-9	104	1.6	93	24.4	14.4	6 219	Antigua and Barbuda
6 800	1 363	6 534	47.1	45 277	92.2	18.2	863	Argentina
43	-2	134	0.7	107	43.9	23.0	0	Aruba
(e) -2 152	279	360	3.2	408	83.4	11.9	72 998	Bahamas
(e) -556	18	239	3.0	281	31.2	23.4	3 253	Barbados
-166	2	128	3.2	400	46.2	7.4	3 822	Belize
815	104	594	0.7	12 079	70.5	7.7	129	Bolivia (Plurinational State of)
..	..	..	..	27	75.1	19.4	..	Bonaire, Sint Eustatius and Saba
-27 925	23 083	50 367	8.3	214 326	87.3	13.7	5 191	Brazil
..	43 217	39 361	3.2	31	48.9	12.6	14	British Virgin Islands

Economy	Merchandise trade			Trade in services		GDP	
	Exports	Imports	Terms of trade	Exports	Imports	Per capita (nominal)	Growth (real)[a]
	(Millions of US$)	(Millions of US$)	(2015=100)	(Millions of US$)	(Millions of US$)	(US$)	(Percentage)
Cayman Islands	(e) 28	1 538	97	-	-	99 007	4.7
Chile	94 677	92 197	136	(e) 6 618	(e) 15 765	16 153	10.7
Colombia	40 287	61 101	126	(e) 6 776	(e) 13 173	6 088	9.9
Costa Rica	15 494	20 728	96	(e) 8 991	(e) 4 624	12 133	5.7
Cuba	(e) 1 498	(e) 8 486	102	-	-	-	2.4
Curaçao	(e) 302	(e) 1 206	100	(e) 812	(e) 436	11 540	-18.4
Dominica	17	231	97	86	99	7 310	3.9
Dominican Republic	(e) 12 462	(e) 24 143	99	8 047	4 398	8 422	11.2
Ecuador	26 699	25 687	107	2 115	4 540	5 883	3.3
El Salvador	6 629	15 076	96	3 106	2 162	4 451	9.4
Falkland Islands (Malvinas)	(e) 298	(e) 151	107	..	..	..	..
Grenada	29	450	86	345	245	8 598	1.4
Guatemala	13 753	26 607	106	2 906	4 214	4 776	5.9
Guyana	4 356	4 376	124	-	-	9 430	19.5
Haiti	(e) 960	(e) 3 232	92	111	618	1 678	-0.9
Honduras	(e) 10 216	(e) 15 040	94	2 550	2 598	2 713	9.4
Jamaica	1 441	5 976	102	(e) 3 001	(e) 2 561	5 264	4.5
Mexico	494 765	522 455	97	(e) 27 312	(e) 38 656	10 089	4.8
Montserrat	8	33	95	6	22	15 806	3.5
Nicaragua	6 495	9 826	101	1 043	855	1 996	5.7
Panama	13 161	20 596	106	10 745	4 263	13 740	10.5
Paraguay	10 547	13 560	146	998	878	5 767	3.7
Peru	59 443	50 871	128	2 947	10 294	6 475	11.2
Saint Barthélemy	..	..	..	..	..	..	..
Saint Kitts and Nevis	50	260	87	382	163	19 303	-1.4
Saint Lucia	59	601	99	826	317	9 883	6.7
Saint Martin (French part)	..	..	109	..	..	..	..
Saint Vincent and the Grenadines	34	373	186	88	88	7 394	-5.3
Sint Maarten (Dutch part)	(e) 141	(e) 785	109	(e) 401	(e) 217	15 207	-24.0
Suriname	1 513	1 381	133	(e) 96	(e) 640	5 164	-0.9
Trinidad and Tobago	8 619	5 763	115	343	2 081	13 956	-1.4
Turks and Caicos Islands	(e) 4	(e) 410	94	-	-	23 488	9.1
Uruguay	9 539	10 320	104	3 776	3 929	17 218	3.7
Venezuela (Bolivarian Rep. of)	(e) 3 575	(e) 7 770	101	-	-	-	2.2
Developing economies: Asia and Oceania	8 148 688	7 371 705	100	1 392 876	1 498 217	6 740	7.0
Afghanistan	(e) 1 037	(e) 5 574	106	-	-	446	4.0
American Samoa	(e) 317	(e) 711	105	-	-	..	..
Armenia	3 023	5 357	108	1 681	1 258	4 945	5.2
Azerbaijan	22 207	11 706	157	3 795	5 918	5 205	4.0
Bahrain	22 369	14 188	112	(e) 13 225	(e) 10 289	26 183	3.2
Bangladesh	44 223	(e) 80 448	83	7 478	10 872	2 155	5.5
Bhutan	784	1 220	151	(e) 82	(e) 221	3 241	-3.4
Brunei Darussalam	11 037	8 570	145	(e) 205	(e) 902	45 436	0.9
Cambodia	17 362	28 369	88	657	2 104	1 612	3.0

| Current account balance | FDI | | CPI growth | Population | | | Fleet size[b] | Economy |
| | Outflows | Inflows | | Total | Share of urban | Old-age dependency ratio | | |
(Millions of US$)	(Millions of US$)	(Millions of US$)	(Percentage)	(Thousands)	(Percentage)	(Percentage)	(1000 of dwt)	
(e) -1 014	21 232	25 893	2.9	68	100.0	10.4	6 070	Cayman Islands
-20 307	12 220	12 719	4.5	19 493	87.8	18.4	981	Chile
-17 892	3 362	9 402	3.5	51 517	81.7	12.5	99	Colombia
-2 106	86	3 196	1.7	5 154	81.4	15.3	3	Costa Rica
-	..	..	255.2	11 256	77.3	22.9	582	Cuba
-	6	154	3.7	190	89.0	21.4	1 365	Curaçao
-179	0	44	0.5	72	71.4	13.2	535	Dominica
-2 689	153	3 102	8.2	11 118	83.2	10.9	68	Dominican Republic
3 060	..	621	0.1	17 798	64.4	11.5	312	Ecuador
-1 457	1	314	3.5	6 314	74.1	12.3	1	El Salvador
..	..	..	..	4	78.9	14.9	6	Falkland Islands (Malvinas)
-294	-6	144	1.2	125	36.7	14.9	1	Grenada
2 177	161	3 472	4.3	17 608	52.2	7.9	2	Guatemala
(e) -1 016	0	1 162	5.1	805	26.9	9.5	973	Guyana
141	..	50	15.9	11 448	58.0	7.1	1	Haiti
-1 385	358	700	4.5	10 278	59.0	6.4	784	Honduras
(e) 109	56	321	5.9	2 828	56.7	10.0	75	Jamaica
-4 866	-717	31 621	5.7	126 705	81.0	12.2	2 202	Mexico
-13	..	1	-0.1	4	9.1	24.7	..	Montserrat
-317	14	1 220	4.9	6 851	59.3	8.0	3	Nicaragua
-1 412	209	1 844	1.6	4 351	68.8	13.2	350 401	Panama
311	..	122	4.8	6 704	62.5	9.6	94	Paraguay
-5 273	188	5 908	4.0	33 715	78.5	12.7	446	Peru
..	..	..	..	11	98.5	13.3	..	Saint Barthélemy
-61	-3	40	0.2	48	30.9	13.7	1 211	Saint Kitts and Nevis
-2	26	47	2.4	180	18.9	12.5	..	Saint Lucia
..	..	..	..	32	98.5	15.6	..	Saint Martin (French part)
-212	4	65	1.6	104	53.5	16.1	2 651	Saint Vincent and the Grenadines
-	6	31	2.8	44	100.0	12.3	..	Sint Maarten (Dutch part)
(e) 149	..	-164	59.1	613	66.2	11.0	7	Suriname
2 506	37	342	1.1	1 526	53.3	15.9	28	Trinidad and Tobago
..	..	29	5.0	45	93.8	13.9	1	Turks and Caicos Islands
-1 092	310	1 646	7.7	3 426	95.6	23.7	60	Uruguay
-	781	-761	1588.5	28 200	88.3	13.1	1 307	Venezuela (Bolivarian Rep. of)
597 942	393 958	619 122	3.7	4 521 430	50.0	13.0	898 908	Developing economies: Asia and Oceania
-	31	21	5.1	40 099	26.3	4.4	..	Afghanistan
..	..	..	..	45	87.2	10.4	..	American Samoa
-511	25	379	7.2	2 791	63.4	19.1	..	Armenia
8 292	77	-1 708	6.7	10 313	56.8	9.7	748	Azerbaijan
(e) 2 602	64	1 766	-0.6	1 463	89.6	4.6	293	Bahrain
-15 563	92	2 896	5.6	169 356	38.9	8.6	4 262	Bangladesh
(e) -282	..	2	8.2	777	43.0	8.6	..	Bhutan
(e) 1 111	..	205	1.5	445	78.6	8.1	462	Brunei Darussalam
-12 339	92	3 484	3.0	16 589	24.7	8.5	427	Cambodia

Economy	Merchandise trade			Trade in services		GDP	
	Exports	Imports	Terms of trade	Exports	Imports	Per capita (nominal)	Growth (real)[a]
	(Millions of US$)	(Millions of US$)	(2015=100)	(Millions of US$)	(Millions of US$)	(US$)	(Percentage)
China	3 363 835	2 688 634	90	(e) 392 198	(e) 441 312	12 132	8.1
China, Hong Kong SAR	669 903	712 358	100	76 763	61 695	49 411	5.7
China, Macao SAR	1 620	19 219	92	(e) 18 370	(e) 3 884	46 322	31.9
China, Taiwan Province of	447 693	382 101	92	52 036	39 562	32 852	5.7
Cook Islands	(e) 22	(e) 136	98	-	-	14 822	-20.0
Fiji	815	2 116	101	284	509	5 307	3.0
French Polynesia	119	1 985	91	-	-	20 201	1.5
Georgia	4 242	10 105	105	(e) 2 546	(e) 1 823	4 883	8.0
Guam	44	(e) 809	121	-	-	..	..
India	395 425	572 909	91	240 657	(e) 195 956	2 253	8.3
Indonesia	229 850	196 041	101	14 033	28 711	4 330	3.6
Iran (Islamic Republic of)	71 646	48 978	138	(e) 5 767	(e) 11 077	16 047	2.8
Iraq	86 298	66 217	107	(e) 4 373	(e) 13 255	4 650	3.9
Jordan	9 357	21 613	99	(e) 4 403	(e) 4 108	4 107	3.1
Kazakhstan	60 625	41 171	133	5 814	7 664	9 935	4.0
Kiribati	9	176	114	-	-	1 581	-0.2
Korea, Dem. People's Rep. of	(e) 131	(e) 490	140	-	-	-	-2.9
Kuwait	63 128	31 889	125	(e) 10 838	(e) 20 675	32 664	3.2
Kyrgyzstan	1 659	5 570	125	(e) 522	(e) 711	1 299	3.6
Lao People's Dem. Rep.	7 695	6 275	170	(e) 125	(e) 252	2 585	2.0
Lebanon	4 590	13 857	104	-	-	-	-15.1
Malaysia	299 028	237 980	105	20 869	35 609	11 027	2.5
Maldives	285	2 574	104	3 665	1 109	8 612	17.9
Marshall Islands	(e) 80	(e) 80	100	-	-	5 957	-1.0
Micronesia (Federated States of)	(e) 71	(e) 197	98	-	-	3 567	-1.8
Mongolia	9 247	6 849	148	(e) 719	(e) 2 051	4 588	4.5
Myanmar	15 145	14 322	127	(e) 2 149	(e) 1 822	916	-21.5
Nauru	(e) 119	(e) 45	101	(e) 14	(e) 45	12 377	1.6
Nepal	1 684	15 893	107	770	1 541	1 223	7.0
New Caledonia	1 696	2 781	129	-	-	35 670	1.5
Niue	1	14	89	-	-	..	..
Northern Mariana Islands	(e) 6	459	129	-	-	..	..
Oman	44 591	30 995	97	-	-	16 328	2.3
Pakistan	28 319	72 515	108	6 498	9 806	1 270	3.8
Palau	2	156	91	(e) 16	(e) 45	13 808	-6.0
Papua New Guinea	10 433	3 024	177	(e) 107	(e) 939	2 538	1.0
Philippines	74 618	124 386	96	33 627	19 453	3 412	4.3
Qatar	87 203	27 985	156	18 346	34 340	69 066	3.5
Samoa	29	368	101	69	92	3 436	-7.8
Saudi Arabia	276 179	152 850	140	10 303	73 281	23 096	3.3
Singapore	457 357	406 226	94	229 866	223 580	64 840	6.0
Solomon Islands	371	(e) 562	93	(e) 50	(e) 156	2 352	1.0
Sri Lanka	12 499	20 637	97	(e) 2 475	(e) 2 953	3 779	3.4
State of Palestine	(e) 2 818	(e) 9 359	68	(e) 894	(e) 1 974	3 290	7.1

| Current account balance | FDI | | CPI growth | Population | | | Fleet size[b] | Economy |
| | Outflows | Inflows | | Total | Share of urban | Old-age dependency ratio | | |
(Millions of US$)	(Millions of US$)	(Millions of US$)	(Percentage)	(Thousands)	(Percentage)	(Percentage)	(1000 of dwt)	
317 301	145 190	180 957	0.9	1 425 893	62.5	19.0	115 154	China
41 712	87 450	140 696	1.6	7 495	100.0	28.7	207 816	China, Hong Kong SAR
(e) 4 127	1 528	-298	0.0	687	100.0	16.9	2	China, Macao SAR
114 681	10 108	5 405	1.8	23 860	79.3	22.4	6 755	China, Taiwan Province of
..	0	8	1.9	17	75.7	17.4	1 817	Cook Islands
-597	35	401	0.2	925	57.7	8.7	73	Fiji
..	1	21	0.5	304	62.1	14.0	26	French Polynesia
-1 834	322	1 153	9.6	3 758	59.9	22.6	8	Georgia
..	..	..	..	171	95.0	18.4	0	Guam
-34 648	15 522	44 735	5.5	1 407 564	35.4	10.1	16 934	India
3 430	3 596	20 081	1.6	273 753	57.3	10.0	29 332	Indonesia
-	82	1 425	40.1	87 923	76.3	10.7	20 195	Iran (Islamic Republic of)
-	135	-2 613	6.0	43 534	71.1	5.8	107	Iraq
(e) -3 444	16	622	1.3	11 148	91.6	5.8	91	Jordan
-5 736	1 468	3 172	8.0	19 196	57.8	12.7	136	Kazakhstan
(e) 35	0	1	3.0		56.3	6.2	367	Kiribati
..	..	18	..	25 972	62.6	16.3	1 105	Korea, Dem. People's Rep. of
(e) 21 734	3 631	198	3.4	4 250	100.0	6.0	4 846	Kuwait
(e) -738	4	248	11.9	6 528	37.1	7.2	..	Kyrgyzstan
(e) -175	..	1 072	3.8	7 425	36.9	6.7	2	Lao People's Dem. Rep.
(e) -4 836	66	273	154.8	5 593	89.1	15.3	188	Lebanon
12 904	4 750	11 620	2.5	33 574	77.7	10.4	9 269	Malaysia
-458	..	443	0.2	521	41.1	6.2	65	Maldives
(e) 8	..	5	3.5	42	78.2	6.8	289 781	Marshall Islands
(e) 3	..	..	2.1	113	23.1	9.3	63	Micronesia (Federated States of)
(e) -2 108	113	2 140	7.1	3 348	68.8	7.0	752	Mongolia
(e) -2 334	..	2 067	6.3	53 798	31.4	9.7	177	Myanmar
..	..	..	1.2	13	100.0	3.9	1	Nauru
-5 379	..	196	3.6	30 035	21.0	9.4	..	Nepal
..	84	-494	0.6	288	71.9	16.0	14	New Caledonia
..	..	..	..	2	46.9	25.4	238	Niue
..	..	..	..	49	91.9	14.3	..	Northern Mariana Islands
(e) -2 438	581	3 619	1.5	4 520	87.0	4.0	20	Oman
-12 262	242	2 102	8.9	231 402	37.4	7.2	868	Pakistan
(e) -122	..	23	0.4	18	81.5	13.7	3 163	Palau
(e) 5 976	-272	87	4.5	9 949	13.5	5.0	199	Papua New Guinea
-6 922	2 402	10 518	3.9	113 880	47.7	8.3	6 201	Philippines
26 288	160	-1 093	2.3	2 688	99.3	1.7	755	Qatar
-116	1	9	-3.0	219	17.7	8.9	1 202	Samoa
44 324	23 860	19 286	3.1	35 950	84.5	3.7	13 887	Saudi Arabia
71 926	47 395	99 099	2.3	5 941	100.0	19.1	131 369	Singapore
(e) -93	-11	50	-0.1	708	25.1	6.0	7	Solomon Islands
-2 266	17	598	6.0	21 773	18.9	17.0	311	Sri Lanka
(e) -1 487	-78	256	1.2	5 133	77.0	6.1	..	State of Palestine

Economy	Merchandise trade			Trade in services		GDP	
	Exports	**Imports**	**Terms of trade**	**Exports**	**Imports**	**Per capita (nominal)**	**Growth (real)[a]**
	(Millions of US$)	(Millions of US$)	(2015=100)	(Millions of US$)	(Millions of US$)	(US$)	(Percentage)
Syrian Arab Republic	739	6 463	88	-	-	-	2.2
Tajikistan	2 150	4 210	136	147	532	830	6.0
Thailand	272 006	266 882	102	24 502	65 501	7 046	0.9
Timor-Leste	616	873	..	(e) 28	(e) 391	1 526	2.1
Tokelau	(e) 0	(e) 0	99	..	..	..	..
Tonga	(e) 16	(e) 276	98	43	72	4 617	-3.2
Türkiye	225 218	271 426	89	58 153	31 602	9 535	11.0
Turkmenistan	9 212	4 026	185	-	-	8 105	5.5
Tuvalu	0	34	-	(e) 7	(e) 36	5 651	3.0
United Arab Emirates	425 160	347 529	-	101 838	76 106	44 663	4.3
Uzbekistan	14 081	23 740	164	2 257	4 723	1 939	6.4
Vanuatu	54	339	102	(e) 36	(e) 124	2 957	1.5
Viet Nam	335 929	331 582	102	3 673	19 407	2 921	1.9
Wallis and Futuna Islands	(e) 0	(e) 74	100	..	..	..	..
Yemen	(e) 662	5 204	131	-	-	1 023	1.2
Selected groups							
Developing economies excluding China	6 553 913	6 578 754	109	1 258 789	1 414 093	4 082	5.6
Developing economies excluding LDCs	9 682 645	8 955 962	103	1 616 315	1 784 435	6 784	6.9
LDCs	235 103	311 426	117	34 672	70 970	1 092	2.0
LLDCs	219 129	250 169	142	36 010	63 589	1 635	4.2
SIDS (UN-OHRLLS)	530 635	514 571	97	286 660	264 557	11 732	5.2
HIPCs (IMF)	176 149	203 532	120	36 479	69 625	1 018	4.1
BRICS	4 657 466	3 914 216	96	731 709	777 032	7 447	7.6
G20	17 066 710	17 367 571	101	4 901 280	4 386 331	16 806	5.9

[a] In constant 2015 United States dollars.
[b] As of 1 January 2022.

| Current account balance | FDI | | CPI growth | Population | | | Fleet size[b] | Economy |
	Outflows	Inflows		Total	Share of urban	Old-age dependency ratio		
(Millions of US$)	(Millions of US$)	(Millions of US$)	(Percentage)	(Thousands)	(Percentage)	(Percentage)	(1000 of dwt)	
(e) -3 526	..	..	98.3	21 324	56.1	7.4	59	Syrian Arab Republic
735	48	84	8.7	9 750	27.7	5.5	..	Tajikistan
-10 582	17 303	11 423	1.2	71 601	52.2	20.8	5 375	Thailand
(e) 42	..	85	3.8	1 321	31.7	8.9	0	Timor-Leste
..	..	..	..	2	0.0	13.4	..	Tokelau
-19	0	2	1.4	106	23.1	10.5	44	Tonga
-13 696	4 979	12 530	19.6	84 775	76.6	12.3	6 257	Türkiye
-	..	1 453	15.0	6 342	53.0	7.7	125	Turkmenistan
(e) 1	..	0	3.0	11	64.8	10.0	2 196	Tuvalu
(e) 47 951	22 546	20 667	0.2	9 365	87.3	2.1	863	United Arab Emirates
-4 810	3	2 044	10.8	34 081	50.4	7.7	..	Uzbekistan
(e) -1	2	26	3.0	319	25.7	6.6	1 749	Vanuatu
-3 812	300	15 660	1.9	97 468	38.1	12.7	12 331	Viet Nam
..	..	..	..	12	0.0	20.4	..	Wallis and Futuna Islands
-	..	..	63.8	32 982	38.5	4.7	419	Yemen
								Selected groups
162 214	293 192	655 614	11.7	5 139 611	48.8	9.5	1 611 749	Developing economies excluding China
534 172	438 524	810 592	5.7	5 465 936	55.1	12.7	1 370 517	Developing economies excluding LDCs
-54 657	-142	25 978	39.3	1 099 569	35.3	6.3	356 386	LDCs
-25 989	1 699	18 486	11.4	550 846	31.6	6.3	2 793	LLDCs
71 484	47 598	107 089	32.9	69 673	60.5	12.1	542 860	SIDS (UN-OHRLLS)
-30 315	2 029	31 695	8.3	811 879	37.6	5.3	351 653	HIPCs (IMF)
392 296	247 417	355 188	2.5	3 252 279	53.1	14.8	148 859	BRICS
390 862	1 495 677	1 103 952	3.7	4 914 238	61.2	17.9	620 125	G20

6.2 Classifications

Classification of economies

UNCTAD's classification of economies into developing and developed is intended for statistical convenience and does not express judgement about the stage reached by a particular country or area in the development process. It is based on the classification applied in the "Standard Country or Area Codes for Statistical Use", known as "M49", maintained by the United Nations Statistics Division (UNSD, 2022). For details, see UNCTAD (2022e). Other international organisations may group economies by development status in slightly different ways. For a comparison of the various groupings in use and their underlying rationales, see Hoffmeister (2020).

Throughout the handbook, the group of developing economies is further broken down into the following three regions: "Africa", the "Americas" and "Asia and Oceania", where the group of African developing economies coincides with Africa, and the group of American developing economies coincides with Latin America and the Caribbean, as defined in the M49 standard (UNSD, 2022). Apart from these five groups of economies, whenever possible data are also presented for the following groups:

- Developing economies excluding China,

- Developing economies excluding LDCs,

- LDCs, according to UN-OHRLLS (2022),

- LLDCs, according to UN-OHRLLS (ibid.),

- SIDS according to UN-OHRLLS (ibid.),

- HIPCs, according to the IMF (2022),

- Brazil, Russia, India, China and South Africa (BRICS),

- Group of Twenty (G20) (Indonesia, 2022).

For SIDS, as for developing and developed economies, different groupings are also applied by international organisations. The definition of SIDS by the UN-OHRLLS, used in the present handbook, is relatively broad. For a comparison and discussion of the different groupings in use, see MacFeely et al. (2021).

The UNCTADstat classification page (UNCTAD, 2022e) provides the lists of the economies included in the different groups of economies above.

Classification of goods

For breakdowns of international merchandise trade by product, UNCTADstat applies the SITC, Revision 3, (UNSD, 1991) and various aggregates compiled on the basis of that classification. In chapter 1 of this handbook, reference is made to the following five product groups:

- All food items (SITC codes 0, 1, 22 and 4),

- Agricultural raw materials (SITC code 2 except 22, 27 and 28),

- Ores, metals, precious stones and non-monetary gold (SITC codes 27, 28, 68, 667 and 971),

- Fuels (SITC code 3),

- Manufactured goods (SITC codes 5, 6, 7 and 8 except 667 and 68).

For the measurement of movements in commodity prices in section 3.4, the UCPI is disaggregated by commodity groups constructed from HS 2007 (World Customs Organization, 2006). For the correspondence between these commodity groups and HS headings and for the individual price quotations represented therein, see UNCTAD (2018).

Classification of services

The breakdown by service category in section 2.2 is based on EBOPS 2010 (United Nations et al., 2012). The EBOPS 2010 main categories have been grouped as shown in table 6.2 below.

Table 6.2 | Grouping of service categories on the basis of EBOPS 2010

EBOPS 2010	Section 2.2
Transport	Transport
Travel	Travel
Insurance and pension services	Insurance, financial, intellectual property, and other business services
Financial services	
Charges for the use of intellectual property n.i.e.	
Other business services	
Telecommunications, computer and information services	Telecommunications, computer and information
Personal, cultural and recreational services	Other categories
Government goods and services n.i.e.	
Construction	
Services not allocated	
Manufacturing services on physical inputs owned by others	
Maintenance and repair services n.i.e.	

Classification of economic activities

In section 3.1, gross value added is broken down by the three broad groups of economic activities below, in accordance with the International Standard Industrial Classification of All Economic Activities (ISIC), Revision 3 (UNSD, 1989):

• Agriculture, comprising: agriculture, hunting, forestry and fishing (ISIC divisions 01 to 05),

• Industry, comprising: mining and quarrying, manufacturing, electricity, gas and water supply, construction (ISIC divisions 10 to 45),

• Services, comprising all other economic activities (ISIC divisions 50 to 99).

6.3 Calculation methods

The **annual average growth rate** over multiple years is calculated in this handbook as least squares growth rate or as exponential growth rate.

The **least squares growth rate** is computed as the coefficient b when fitting the regression model

$$ln\,(y_{t+i}) = a + bi \quad \text{for} \quad i \in \{0, 1, 2, ..., k\}$$

with least squares, where k stands for the length of the time period (in years), t for the base year, and y represents the object of measurement. This method takes all observations in the analyzed period into account.

The **exponential growth rate** is calculated as $\quad b = \dfrac{1}{k} \cdot ln\left(\dfrac{y_{t+k}}{y_t}\right)$

Throughout the handbook, the growth rates of monetary values are based on current prices, unless otherwise specified.

The **trade openness index** (map 1.4) is calculated as the ratio of the arithmetic mean of merchandise exports (x) and imports (m) to GDP (y):

$$TOI_{i,t} = \frac{\frac{1}{2}(x_{i,t} + m_{i,t})}{y_{i,t}}$$

where i designates the economy and t the year.

The **terms of trade index** (figure 1.4.1, tables 1.4.1 and 1.4.2) with base year 2015 is calculated as follows:

$$ToT_{i,t} = 100 \, \frac{\dfrac{UVI_{exports,i,t}}{UVI_{imports,i,t}}}{\dfrac{UVI_{exports,i,2015}}{UVI_{imports,i,2015}}}$$

where $UVI_{exports,i,t}$ is the unit value index of exports and $UVI_{imports,i,t}$ the unit value index of imports of economy i at time t.

The **market concentration index of exports** (figure 1.4.2) is calculated as a normalized Herfindahl-Hirschmann index:

$$MCI_{exports,i} = \frac{\sqrt{\sum_{j=1}^{n} \left(\frac{x_{i,j}}{X_i}\right)^2} - \sqrt{\frac{1}{n}}}{1 - \sqrt{\frac{1}{n}}}, \quad \text{with} \quad X_i = \sum_{j=1}^{n} x_{i,j}$$

where $x_{i,j}$ is the value of exports of product i from economy j and n is the number of economies.

The **product concentration index of exports** (figure 1.4.3) is calculated as a normalized Herfindahl-Hirschmann index:

$$PCI_{exports,j} = \frac{\sqrt{\sum_{i=1}^{n} \left(\frac{x_{i,j}}{X_j}\right)^2} - \sqrt{\frac{1}{n}}}{1 - \sqrt{\frac{1}{n}}}, \quad \text{with} \quad X_j = \sum_{i=1}^{n} x_{i,j},$$

where $x_{i,j}$ is the value of exports of product i from economy j and n is the number of product groups according to SITC, Revision 3, at the 3-digit level.

The **volume index of exports (imports)** (figure 1.4.3, tables 1.4.1 and 1.4.2) is calculated by dividing the export (import) value index by the corresponding unit value index and scaling up by 100:

$$QI_{i,t} = 100 \, \frac{VI_{i,t}}{UVI_{i,t}}$$

where $VI_{i,t}$ is the value index of exports (imports), given by

$$VI_{i,t} = 100 \, \frac{x_{i,t}}{x_{i,2015}}$$

$x_{i,t}$ is the value of exports (imports), $UVI_{i,t}$ is the unit value index of exports (imports), i designates the economy and t the time period.

The **purchasing power index of exports** (table 1.4.1 and 1.4.2) is calculated by dividing the export value index by the corresponding import unit value index and scaling up by 100:

$$PPI_{exports,i,t} = 100 \, \frac{VI_{exports,i,t}}{UVI_{imports,i,t}}$$

where $VI_{exports,i,t}$ is the value index of exports (as defined above), $UVI_{imports,i,t}$ is the unit value index of imports, i designates the economy and t the time period.

The **Lorenz curve** in figure 3.1.3 plots cumulative population shares ordered by GDP per capita, on the x-axis, against the cumulative shares of global GDP which they account for, on the y-axis. For the construction of the Lorenz curve, the n economies of the world are ordered with reference to their GDP per capita, so that

$$\frac{y_i}{p_i} \geq \frac{y_{i-1}}{p_{i-1}} \text{ for all } i \in \{2, 3, ..., n\}$$

where y_i is GDP and p_i the population of the economy at position i in this ranking, counted from below.

The cumulative population shares, measured on the x-axis, are calculated as

$$P_i = \sum_{j=1}^{i} \frac{p_j}{p} \quad \text{with } p = p_1 + p_2 + ... + p_n$$

The cumulative shares of global GDP, measured on the y-axis, are calculated as follows:

$$Y_i = \sum_{j=1}^{i} \frac{y_j}{y} \quad \text{with } y = y_1 + y_2 + ... + y_n$$

The **UNCTAD Commodity Price Index** (section 3.4) is a fixed base-weight Laspeyres index with base year 2015=100. It is calculated as

$$L_t = \frac{\sum_{i=1}^{n} p_{i,t} \, q_{i,2015}}{\sum_{i=1}^{n} p_{i,2015} \, q_{i,2015}}$$

where i is the identifier of the commodity group, $q_{i,2015}$ is the quantity in which products of commodity group i were exported by developing economies during the three years around the base year (from 2014 to 2016), and $p_{i,t}$ is the price of a representative product, within commodity group i, in year t. For more details, see UNCTAD (2018).

6.4 References

Hoffmeister O (2020). Development status as a measure of development. UNCTAD Research Paper No. 46. UNCTAD.

IMF (2009). Balance of Payments and International Investment Position Manual. Washington D.C.

IMF (2022). Debt relief under the Heavily Indebted Poor Countries (HIPC) Initiative. Available at https://www.imf.org/en/About/Factsheets/Sheets/2016/08/01/16/11/Debt-Relief-Under-the-Heavily-Indebted-Poor-Countries-Initiative (accessed 10 November 2022).

Indonesia (2022). G20 Presidency of Indonesia. Recover together. Recover stronger. Available at https://g20.org (accessed 10 November 2022).

MacFeely S, Hoffmeister O, Barnat N, Hopp D and Peltola A (2021). Constructing a criteria-based classification for Small Island Developing States: an investigation. UNCTAD Research Paper No. 66. UNCTAD.

UN DESA (2018). World Urbanization Prospects. The 2018 revision: Methodology. ESA/P/WP/252. New York.

UN DESA (2019). World Urbanization Prospects 2018: Highlights. United Nations publication. Sales No. E19.XIII.6. New York.

UN DESA (2022a). World Population Prospects 2022: Summary of Results. United Nations publication. Sales No. E.22.XIII.3. New York.

UN DESA (2022b). World Population Prospects 2022: Methodology of the United Nations population estimates and projections. UN DESA/POP/2022/TR/NO. 4. New York.

UNCTAD (2018). UNCTAD Commodity Price Index. Methodological note. UNCTAD/STAT/CPB/MN/1. Geneva. Available at https://unctad.org/system/files/official-document/statcpbmn1_en.pdf (accessed 7 November 2022).

UNCTAD (2022a). UNCTADstat. Available at https://unctadstat.unctad.org/EN/Index.html (accessed 1 October 2022).

UNCTAD (2022b). UNCTAD Nowcasts. Available at https://unctadstat.unctad.org/EN/Nowcasts.html (accessed 11 October 2022).

UNCTAD (2022c). World Investment Report 2022: International Tax Reforms and Sustainable Investment. United Nations publication. Sales No. E.21.II.D.20. New York and Geneva.

UNCTAD (2022d). Review of Maritime Transport 2022. United Nations publication. Sales No. E.22.II.D.42. New York and Geneva.

UNCTAD (2022e). UNCTADStat: Classifications. Available at https://unctadstat.unctad.org/EN/Classifications.html (accessed 1 October 2022).

United Nations (2011). International Merchandise Trade Statistics: Concepts and Definitions 2010. United Nations publication. Sales No. E.10.XVII.13. New York.

United Nations et al. (2012). Manual on Statistics of International Trade in Services 2010. United Nations publication. Sales No. E.10.XVII.14. Geneva.

United Nations (2022). UN Comtrade Database. Available at https://comtrade.un.org/ (accessed 1 November 2022).

United Nations, European Commission, IMF, OECD, and World Bank (2009). System of National Accounts 2008. United Nations publication. Sales No. E.08.XVII.29. New York.

UN-OHRLLS (2022). Office of the High Representative for the Least Developed Countries, Landlocked Developing Countries and Small Island Developing States. Available at https://www.un.org/ohrlls/ (accessed 10 November 2022).

UNSD (1989). International Standard Industrial Classification of All Economic Activities. Revision 3. United Nations publication. Sales No. E.90.XVII.11. New York.

UNSD (1991). Standard International Trade Classification, Rev. 3. Statistical papers, No. ST/ESA/STAT/SER.M/34/Rev.3. United Nations publication. Sales No. E.86.XVII.12. New York.

UNSD (2022). Standard country or area codes for statistical use (M49). Available at https://unstats.un.org/unsd/methodology/m49/ (accessed 11 October 2022).

World Customs Organization (2006). Amendments to the Harmonized System Nomenclature. Effective from 1 January 2007. Brussels.